OUTRAGE

Canada's Justice System on Trial

Alex Macdonald

RAINCOAST BOOKS

Vancouver

First published in 1999 by
RAINCOAST BOOKS
8680 Cambie Street
Vancouver, B.C.
V6P 6M9
(604) 323-7100

1 2 3 4 5 6 7 8 9 10

Canadian Cataloguing In Publication Data
Macdonald, Alex, 1918-
Outrage
ISBN 1-55192-230-4
1. Criminal justice, Administration of--Canada. I. Title.
KE8813.M32 1999   345.71'05   C98-911174-1
KF9223.M32. 1999

Interior Design by Andrew Johnstone

THE CANADA COUNCIL | LE CONSEIL DES ARTS
FOR THE ARTS | DU CANADA
SINCE 1957 | DEPUIS 1957

Raincoast Books gratefully acknowledges the support of the Government
of Canada, through the Book Publishing Industry Development Program,
the Canada Council and the Department of Canadian Heritage. We also
acknowledge the assistance of the Province of British Columbia, through
the British Columbia Arts Council.

Printed in Canada

Contents

To my ever-supportive wife, Dorothy

Acknowledgements

I must thank those who helped me in the creation of this work, especially Elizabeth Godley, who threw back at me stale verbiage, creaky jargon and other incomprehensibles. Alan Frantz, an eminent and able B.C. provincial prosecutor, read the manuscript and caught me up on some of my lapses. I am still not quite certain what Brian Scrivener of Raincoast Books did with the manuscript, but I do know his contribution made for a better book.
My apologies and thanks to anyone I have left out.
Any errors, omissions or follies remaining are mine alone.

Preface

C anada's legal system is heading for disaster, so preoccupied with protecting individuals' rights that it fails to protect the rights of society. More than fair to a few, the legal system is less than fair to the majority of Canadians, sacrificing time-honoured concepts such as Truth and Justice to an unhealthy fascination with process.

That our legal system is a cornerstone of democracy almost goes without saying. And when the courts are working efficiently, few begrudge the cost. Each year, Canadians pay untold billions to oil the wheels of Justice – as much as, if not more than, we spend to support all of our public schools. And that sum does not begin to take into account the consequences of crime – in shattered lives, injuries, emotional trauma, anxiety and grief, property losses, beefed-up security, court personnel and corrections facilities.

No one among us would question the need for a fair and judicious judicial system, nor would we begrudge cost. But when our legal system bogs down in legalistic nit-picking and lawyerly zealotry – adding nothing to the administration of justice but ratcheting up the costs – Canadians are right to ask for what, exactly, are we paying through the nose?

After looking at crime statistics south of the border, we in this country often feel fortunate that life is safer here. Nevertheless, each year, Canadians face a one-in-four chance of being victimized by some criminal act. Should you live only to the unripe age of 60, you have a 99-percent chance of suffering a crime against your person or property. Should you be an unmarried woman, you have seven times the average odds of suffering violent victimization.[1]

Nowadays, too many citizens are feeling alienated, distrustful and disrespectful of their criminal justice system. Is it any wonder, when even a minute sampling of the hundreds of rulings made by our judges, reveals the following?

- A report is leaked. In it, the chief of British Columbia's provincial court system (it could be any province) speaks of overwhelming caseloads and says that "unless drastic steps are taken, thousands of prosecutions will have to be 'stayed' and some very serious crimes will go unpunished. We are close to a disaster hitting us."[2]

- A conference marking the sixteenth anniversary of the Charter of Rights is held in Ontario in 1998. A legal scholar offers the sobering conclusion that "the criminal decisions of the Supreme Court of Canada are barely comprehensible." A distinguished prosecutor adds that, "Every time I go to the Supreme Court, I haven't a clue what will happen; flipping a coin is not a bad way to proceed."[3]

- In Kamloops, British Columbia, again in 1998, a petty theft is committed. An officer asks a young man walking in the area for his name. He refuses to give it and is arrested for obstructing a peace officer. Then the young man attempts to run away. Now he is charged with both obstruction and escape from custody. At trial he is convicted, but when his appeal goes to the B.C. Supreme Court, a judge cites a Supreme Court of Canada precedent in ruling that the young man was under no legal duty to give his name, only a "moral or social duty to assist police." Why do we allow such a wide gap to spread between a plain moral and social duty and what the law calls for?

- An Asian gang member is ordered deported from Canada. Two years later, in 1997, taking advantage of our legal appeal procedures, he is still in the country, doing business as usual, where he becomes the prime suspect in a horrifying hit-and-run that killed his gang leader's baby.

These are only a few examples of the madness that has gripped our courts. When even those in the highest positions warn of impending disaster, is it any wonder average citizens feel not only alienated, but powerless? Many of us feel that we are bereft of any ability to influence the course of justice within our legal system. As if the Law were the private purview of lawyers. As if the Law were over our heads, and we citizens should not bother ourselves about it.

What has driven us so far off course? I lay the blame squarely on Canada's Charter of Rights and Freedoms, adopted in 1982. Of course, there is much that's good in the Charter, which enshrines such fundamental liberties as freedom of expression and equal rights. But the Charter's legal rights section has ill-served the cause of fair and expeditious justice. Indeed, its effect has been to raise the rights of accused persons too far above the rights of victims and communities. These rights are couched in vague language, susceptible to differing interpretations and judgements. Subsequent legal precedents have placed too little importance on the responsibilities that should fall on all citizens if the law is not to be viewed as a complete ass.

The Charter can also be faulted for the "Americanization" of our justice system. No longer do Canadians look smugly south of the border and say, "That couldn't happen here." Too much of it *is* happening here. On both sides of the 49th Parallel, the balance is tilting against law enforcement and public safety in favour of the privacy and other rights of possible offenders. Just look at the protracted search for the perpetrators of the Air India disaster, which has been hobbled by procedural obstacles for more than a decade.

Yes, the legendary scales, held aloft by the figure of Lady Justice in her flowing robes, are unbalanced. Unfortunately, the good woman's blindfold prevents her from seeing what goes on in our courtrooms.

Trenchant reforms in criminal justice procedure are what is needed. But they will not come easily. The vast legal establishment is deeply conservative and famously resistant to change. Legal institutions have solidified into self-serving industries, and those people whose living depends on them have a vested interest in what is, not what ought to be.

When it comes to changing our ways, the advice of the legal community must, of course, be taken seriously. Therefore, this book will speak to the estimable and hard-working judges, attorneys, peace officers and court staff, working at all levels of the justice system, with appreciation to those judges and parliamentarians who are striving for legal reform, sometimes with success, limited though it may be. But our crisis is too daunting to be left primarily to those who got us into it in the first place.

Even without a law degree, each citizen has the right – and the smarts – to decide how well or how poorly the Law is working. Ordinary Canadians, now too estranged from their own laws, must have a say. Sensible, informed argument is the only remedy against the demagogues clamouring for longer jail terms and bigger prisons. We must never forget that the United States, the least safe of Western countries, boasts the highest rate of incarceration.

Of course, what has been termed the State's "awesome power" must be countered with concern for offenders' rights. Such power can indeed be tyrannical, although seldom in countries well nurtured in the traditions of British common law.

Some will ask what qualifies me to sit in judgement on these matters, to challenge the weighty volumes of precedents and procedures arrayed on library shelves. I will reply that I, well into the age of immodesty, have seen and heard a thing or two in my career as a lawyer in every kind of Canadian court, high and low. For 39 years, I handled cases for many citizens, some of whom were badly confused, some of them stupid, some simply unlucky. Some faced charges of murder, some drunk driving.

But long before that 39-year career began, I was destined for the Law, begotten and bred for it. At the knee of my father, who served as Chief Justice of British Columbia, I was still in knickers when I first heard law talk. My elder brother, an appeal court justice, has been heard to say he never lost a case after being made a judge. I myself was offered a judgeship but turned it down, explaining that my attention span was too long.

During my active service in B.C.'s courtrooms, I took time out to serve as the province's Attorney-General from 1972-75, occupying the same office and chair that my father had a half-century earlier – although, unlike him, I entered from the left wing.

More recently, rehabilitated after my political career, I have become a part-time professor, with a teaching position at Simon Fraser University. Now provided a perch with a panoramic view, I no longer have to fret about making a law practice pay, and I hope not vainly I can inject a dose of Scottish common sense into the proceedings.

My love-affair with the law began some three-score years ago in classes at Toronto's Osgoode Hall, whence I graduated in 1946. While there, I fell for the Law's high ideals: to follow truth wherever it led; to use reason in the resolution of human conflicts; to attempt, however hamfistedly, to bring order, correction and discipline into what would otherwise be a chaotic society.

At the same time, the Law's historic traditions cast a spell on me. I loved the learning, dignity and incorruptibility of its judges and the ceremonious decorum of its courtrooms.

I still revere the grand and meaningful liberties, so hard-won in the evolution of the Common Law – to be free to do whatever is not prohibited by clear and valid law; to be brought before a judge by habeas corpus within hours of arrest; to confront one's accusers in open court; to be guilty only if so found beyond a reasonable doubt; to not be subjected to cruel and unusual punishment; and so on.

However, I also feel a strong need to try to right what is amiss in our laws. Never one to shirk a seemingly impossible task, I have decided to spend my dotage identifying the flaws in our criminal justice system and proposing strategies for their repair. And so this book, a child of my later years – almost abandoned after a break-in of my car when my zippered note-case, containing all my laborious work, was stolen, along with my squash racquet. Fortunately, fate was kind. After receiving a telephoned invitation to a welfare hotel, I met with two drifters, one a Newfie, the other from the Lakehead, who told me they had found my note-case in a back-alley trash can. (Sadly, my racquet never has turned up.) The $35 tip they extracted for returning my manuscript was a small price to pay, and I left them feeling that criminals are more like you and me than we like to believe.

But I digress. Sadly, my early illusions about the Law have suffered somewhat, and now I see, with jaundiced eyes, a growing gap between those lofty ideals and its performance, especially in the criminal justice system. Too often the pursuit of truth is handicapped by legalistic objections. Barren technicalities derail common sense without advancing liberty, individual or general. Investigations and trials get snared in the web of spun-out complexities. The quest for truth has deteriorated into a mere game, with the main beneficiaries the well-paid players.

Surely my old flame the Law cannot be drifting into irrelevance? No. I firmly believe that with the proper treatment, she can still be of practical help to people in their daily lives, and this in turn will encourage citizens to hold her in the esteem she should enjoy.

So, with this goal in mind, I will attempt to untangle the law's complexities and demystify its process by presenting the facts – actual cases, not speculation. And I've tried not to stack the deck. The examples I've chosen come from widely reported trials from across our country and illustrate the impact of our criminal processes on everyday life. By reading these tales – often tragic, occasionally amusing and always interesting – you, Dear Reader, will be able to see what needs to be done, with little need of assistance from me.

Your empowerment is crucial, because woven through this book is an important thread – the principle that citizens must take responsibility for mending our out-of-whack legal apparatus. That's one of the costs of living in a free and democratic society. Only an informed and determined public can spark the revolution that will save our criminal justice system from a catastrophic breakdown.

Chapter 1

Anything But the Truth

"No one 'ere feared
that the truth should heared,
but they whom the truth would indict."

– Robert Burns

The Charter was still a newborn babe when our highest court began to swaddle it in some of the tattiest hand-me-downs of U.S. criminal law. First, the Court took the Charter provision that anyone arrested must be told he or she is entitled to a lawyer and extended it to situations where a lawyer's advice wouldn't be of any use to the accused. Then, to make matters worse, the Court decided that the way to guarantee that suspects were given this right was to throw out the evidence against them if they weren't. As if this were the only way to ensure that the Charter was lived up to! This was an ominous beginning to the grand project of Charter interpretation. It over-turned long-established Canadian law that allowed courts and juries to look at all relevant and reliable evidence, with the exception of confessions that had been elicited by threats or promises.

Taking this path has led us into brave new Charter territory, where procedural improprieties weigh as much in the scales of justice as do considerations of guilt or innocence. In this post-Charter world, trials are a game in which each side must live with its mistakes, even if this skews the outcome, and where protecting the adversarial process is as important as bringing out the truth.

One Too Many

A respectable employee of the City of Moose Jaw, Paul Therens was a moderate social drinker who'd never had any brushes with the law. However, on the night of April 25, 1982, he drove off the road and into a tree. It wasn't much of an accident. Paul had been driving with *too much* care and attention, alternately checking out the curbs and centre line, steering warily. The only damage – to the car, at least – was a broken headlight and smashed fender. The real damage was to come in the precedents his case set, precedents that have reverberated through the justice system, causing legal havoc.

When the police arrived and asked that he accompany them to the station, Therens did as he was requested. When they asked him to blow into the breathalyzer, he politely acquiesced, easily exceeding the permissible limit. He neither asked for a lawyer nor indicated he wanted one. Indeed, Therens stood visibly in greater need of a nurse or a divine. It was as if he were challenging the ingenuity of any court in the land to find him not guilty. The Supreme Court of Canada rose to his challenge. (*R v Therens*, 1985, SCC 18 CCC (3rd) 481).

In acquitting him, the Court took several wrong turns. First, it recited Section 10(b), known as the "lawyers' section" of the Charter: "Anyone detained or arrested has the right: ... (b) To retain and instruct counsel without delay and to be informed of that right."

It's true that the police neglected to tell Therens he could talk to a lawyer before standing up to the breathalyzer. It mattered not that all a lawyer could have told him was what any driver should know anyway. That is, by law, he had to blow. Had he not done so, he would have committed a criminal offence. Kindly forget that some errant lawyers advise against a blow, figuring a bad reading will make it harder for their client to win a civil damage suit or defend against one. (Such scoundrels should be disbarred for advocating law-breaking.) Not that these lawyers lack legal smarts. Many a misbehaving driver, advised not to blow, has wrung some compensating damages from an insurance company anxious to avoid the greater costs of a court defence.

The Court, however, was not to be put off by such mundane practicalities. It found a Charter breach, "given the importance of the right to counsel," and decided Therens's breathalyzer reading had to be excluded. It would not be fitting to suggest that the Court was actuated by a laudable desire to keep the legal profession busy.

But the *Therens* matter raised another question. Did the Court really have to find that Therens had been "arrested or detained"? After all, he was not charged until after his test; he had gone freely to the station house, and even if police had to take him there, it was because the law said he must attend. If his breath hadn't been so thick, he would have been sent home in a taxi. Did the "lawyers' section" have to be interpreted to make it harder to get at the facts during the investigating stage of a possible court case?

Take the Charter word "detained." When is one detained? Let's suppose a burly lawman looks down his nose at you and growls, "Walk this way." You are indisputably under some pressure to obey, though you probably won't succeed in imitating his lumbering gait. You trot after him to his cruiser, and on to the station house, for a breath check and a little chat. Perhaps even a polygraph. You've been "detained," all right.

Yet daily, people are "detained" and investigated as often by the heavy hand of their employer as by the heavy hand of the State. Take the matter of one John Chafie, who was thought to be the one skimming off fees in a parkade. His employer hired a private investigator and told Chafie to go see him and tell him all he knew. Chafie did so. How could he refuse if he valued his job, or worse, needed it?

For his troubles, he was, through psychological coercion, "detained." No lawyer turned up to warn him, "Don't answer that question" or "Don't empty your pockets." What the private eye wormed out of him got Chafie convicted of theft, though he stood in greater need of "rights" than Therens ever did. Eventually, the Ontario Court of Appeal affirmed that Chafie had been detained by a private person, but that here the Charter rights did not apply. (*R v Chafie,* 1985, Ont. C.A., 47 CCC (3rd) 27.)

Why not? Justice Krever, for the Court, said that to apply Charter rights to Chafie's predicament would result in "the judicialization of private relationships beyond the point that society could tolerate; that advice about the right to counsel must be given by a school teacher to a pupil, by an employer to an employee, by a parent to a child, is difficult to contemplate."

Still, the Court did have a problem here. These Charter words are broad as well as misguided, failing to make a clear distinction between the investigative and prosecutorial stages. It is possible to protect individual rights yet still make such a distinction. Americans differentiate between the evidence-gathering and court-process stages – at least in their Constitution, if not in its application. Their counterpart to our "lawyers' section" is the Sixth Amendment to their Bill of Rights, which reads:

> "In all criminal prosecutions the accused shall enjoy the right...to have the assistance of counsel for his defence."

There is, therefore, no American constitutional right to a lawyer during ongoing investigations, including tests of breath, urine or blood, fingerprinting, line-ups and so on. The right accrues once an accused is confronted with the arcane rules of pre-trial and trial procedures. It was to that trial stage that a U.S. Supreme Court Judge referred when he wrote:

> "An accused should have counsel in all cases of serious crime, where there is a danger of conviction because he does not know how to establish his innocence." [1]

In Canada, the *Therens* decision had moved the right to a lawyer to the time of arrest or detention. In doing so, it caught up with and passed American law in its interference with the ascertainment of the truth. It exalted suspects' rights at the expense of public safety.

Then the Court took a second, and surprising, wrong turn, without even so much as using a turn-signal, when it decided that Therens's breathalyzer reading had to be expunged. In doing so, the Court decided to condone Therens's crime, rather than condone the police officer's honest mistake – if it could even be called a mistake, in natural justice.

Lawyer First, Facts Later

The shift in the law that let Therens walk free had occurred fairly recently. Years ago, all trustworthy evidence was taken into account throughout the English-speaking world. [2] Then, in Arizona in 1964, a culprit called Ernesto Miranda kidnapped and raped an 18-year-old girl. She picked him out of a line-up and he was interrogated for two hours, ending with a confession. In

Court, however, it emerged that Miranda had not been told of his right to a lawyer, and that the questioning had been abusive and coercive. Although everyone knew Miranda was guilty as charged, the U.S. Supreme Court cleared him, saying that "he had not been informed of his Constitutional rights."[3]

Many Americans were not impressed with this reasoning, including their preeminent authority on evidence, J. H. Wigmore. Sardonically, this learned gentleman referred to the situation as "upholding the Constitution by not striking at the man that broke it, but letting off someone else who broke something else."[4]

Some of the Miranda virus infected our 1982 Charter – Section 24(2), for example, which reads:

> "...the evidence shall be excluded if it is established that, hav-
> ing regard to all the circumstances, the admission of it would
> bring the administration of justice into disrepute."

The drafters intended this to be a classic Canadian compromise between the restrictive American exclusionary rules and our unrestricted consideration of probative evidence. And so it would have been, had the word "disrepute" been give its plain meaning. Any handy dictionary will tell you it means general public disesteem – in other words, getting a bad reputation amongst friends and neighbours.

In the *Therens* case, Justice William McIntyre, the lone dissenter, sensibly wrote:

> "The *exclusion* of the evidence in this case would go far to bring
> the administration of justice into disrepute." [emphasis added]

The Court majority, however, preferred to get bogged down in arcane legal concepts, deciding that Therens's breath had been "self-conscripted" – a strange offspring of the "right to silence" – and that the breath evidence was not "real" – although a crimson nose, glassy eyes and slurred speech presumably is. On this basis, the Court decided that "the fairness" – in other words, the lawfulness – of the trial had been compromised.

Justice Estey, one of the majority, concluded by saying that unless the evidence was rejected: "The Court would be inviting the police to disregard Charter rights with impunity; and, the Court must avoid the taint of official lawlessness."

Estey went on to describe the conduct of the officers who detained Therens as "flagrant" and "overt." Overt it was, but flagrant? Emphatically not! By all accounts they were the very souls of politeness.

If the Learned Judge still thinks excluding reliable evidence amends police behaviour for the better, let him look south of the line. No justice system suppresses truth on technicalities more than the American system does. And no police forces, in any Western democracy, resort to brutalities and deception more often than do the American.

Surely there are more effective ways to ensure that police and prosecutors play by the rules, fairly and lawfully, than by refusing to admit evidence. Rules of conduct, disciplinary tribunals, careful recruitment and training, continuing education and liability for civil damage suits can all play a role.

But the Court, by taking this Charter section as a virtually absolute exclusionary rule, really set the cat amongst the pigeons. The Therens decision led the Court off the terra firma of sensible social policy into a quicksand swamp. Innumerable hours of court time would be spent looking for Charter lapses to suppress perfectly good evidence. Drunken drivers would walk at a cost in lives, injuries, hospital bills – not to mention the justice system's good name. Murderers, too, would walk. Thoughtful citizens wondered if we were not paying too steep a price by burying evidence in order to send a questionably effective message to police forces to get their act together.

Therens – or any other person, inebriated or sober, who gets behind the wheel – does not have a right to drive. In our society, driving is a privilege, subject to good behaviour on the roads and, on occasion, a breathalyzer test. Had Therens been "detained" in a roadside screening, his breath would have been taken lawfully, without benefit of legal counsel. Was the police-station test so different that a lawyer was required – a lawyer who should only have said, "Blow! I'll see you in the morning"?

The Supreme Court had stretched the word "detained" to cover far too much territory. Peace officers in their daily work have to "detain" citizens in many situations – looking for leads, determining whether an offence has been committed, checking drivers at roadblocks for seat belts and, more often, sobriety. To say these duties, without "lawyering" the detainee, amount to a constitutional violation, is absurd.

After *Therens,* dismayed Ontario prosecutors sought to legalize roadblocks before their Court of Appeal. They amassed evidence on road-related carnage, quoting figures from Statistics Canada showing how drinking driving had contributed, between 1983 and 1991, to 17,630 deaths, 1,075,000 bodily injuries, 327,660 hospital stays and to more than 5 million lost work days. The Appeal Court responded to their pleas by wriggling around.[5] Later, the Supreme Court, in a different case, rather sheepishly upheld the ruling.[6]

Some of *Therens's* Offspring

Like a pebble tossed into a pond, the *Therens* case continues to affect legal decision-making. One of *Therens's* early offspring was a Mr. Mohl, of Saskatoon, who was pulled over by the RCMP for "erratic" driving. At the jailhouse, Mohl received the benefit of the full recitation of his Charter rights. He badly flunked the breathalyzer, but the Court of Appeal later held that he was so thoroughly intoxicated that he didn't know what his Chartering officer had been talking about. On this basis he was acquitted. Drunkenness *could* be a defence to drunk driving. Justice Wakeling, however, dissented, and in full command of his faculties upbraided Mohl for his "self-induced intoxication." He also praised the officers involved (who were required to test Mohl within two hours of his being stopped), saying they had "done the best they could in the circumstances." [7]

Another child of *Therens* was the case of Patrick Prosper. Patrick had been weaving a stolen car down the streets of Halifax until, alerted by a police siren, he fled on foot. He was finally captured, unsteady on his feet and slurred in his speech, and transported to the station, where a patient officer helped him make 15 calls to various legal-aid lawyers. But it was Saturday afternoon, and they must all have been on the golf course. Prosper then took the breathalyzer, sending it into its upper registers. Somehow, Prosper's impaired conviction made it to Ottawa. The Court decided that the police could have held off the test still longer. Prosper's conviction was set aside.[8]

In a spirited dissent, Madam Justice L'Heureux-Dubé wrote that this decision "sounded the death-knell of breathalyzer tests unless provinces provided round-the-clock legal aid"; that "the availability of legal aid is not for the courts to decide"; and that "the inevitable result will be death and carnage on the roads in provinces not making legal aid available at night and on weekends."

Another *Therens* beneficiary, if that's the word, was Mr. Bartle, a resident of Hamilton, who with lots of help from his lawyer raised the prosecutor's high-jump bar a notch or two. Bartle came a cropper in the wee hours one morning after he took evasive action by way of a U-turn to avoid a road check. A constable, nevertheless, apprehended him, smelled his breath, which was redolent of spirits, and Chartered him at the station.

Before taking the breathalyzer test, which he failed, Bartle was asked by both the officer and the breathalyzer technician if he wanted a lawyer. Both times, he said "No." But he was not told there was a 24-hour duty counsel with a 1-800 number he could call. This, the Supreme Court ruled, was a flaw fatal to his impaired conviction.

The ever-sensible Madam Justice L'Heureux-Dubé thought otherwise. She pointed out (together with Justice Gonthier) that the Charter did not require the officer to give his inebriated catch the 1-800 number. 'It does now,' was the riposte of her seven colleagues. [9]

Then there was the lawyer in Kingston, Ontario, who refused the breathalyzer while he communed for 20 minutes on the phone with another lawyer. [10] This tried the patience of a police officer, who was finally able to test the first of two required samples (a test which the lawyer failed) before the second lawyer arrived on the scene. The test of the second sample, taken with both lawyers present, also failed. After all this, the officer's forbearance was once more put to the test when the lawyer he'd arrested was let off by a provincial judge who faulted the officer's impatience, saying that the rights of the accused had been violated "in the extreme." I leave analysis of that interpretation to the reader.

Yet another case tainted by *Therens* is that of Gail St. Pierre. In 1992, she was waiting in line for her breath test. Twice, she repaired to the ladies' washroom, where she knocked off the small bottle of vodka she had in her purse. After failing her test, she explained that she had merely taken the swigs of alcohol to "calm her nerves." The Supreme Court excluded the test evidence as too removed from driving time. [11]

A forlorn-sounding Madam L'Heureux-Dubé again dissented, speaking of "absurd results." She came close to quoting Don Quixote: "Why do you lead me a wild-goose chase?"

These decisions have had one major effect – fewer impaired drivers plead guilty. Their cases overburden provincial courts. The ingenuity of defence counsel seems inexhaustible. For instance, how about this one: "My client was too drunk to understand the police caution." Or the so-called "Liars' Defence," where drinking buddies are found to have carefully counted the ounces imbibed by the accused. Oh yes, there are any number of fashionable ploys, shared amongst defence counsel.

In Vancouver, a 1994 study showed that only 23 percent of impaired charges resulted in convictions. An article in *The Vancouver Sun,* March 25, 1995, quoted a Vancouver defence lawyer boasting of winning 80 percent of his impaired-drivers' cases, as well as a police supervisor who added that, "There is only an 0.02 percent chance of being caught if you drink and drive." It's easy to imagine why disheartened patrol officers too often simply give roadside suspensions and advice to take a taxi home, while another large shade tree grows between Justice and the light of Truth.

Even the question of when an officer can call for a breath test is increasingly a vexing matter. Consider Peter Kain, a West Vancouver businessman, who, at 2 a.m. one November morning in 1996, drove his Jaguar into False Creek. Trapped in the car, his lady companion drowned.

Testimony revealed that Kain had come from an extended dinner, with wine galore. His breath, an officer testified, "smelled of alcohol" and his eyes were glazed. He refused to blow, not allowing the breathalyzer to measure either his sobriety or lack thereof. Nevertheless, a provincial court judge, citing precedent, dismissed all charges, referring to Kain's emotional state and saying the accident "might" have been caused by "cruise-control" malfunction. The officer's "reasonable belief" that Kain was three sheets to the wind was overruled. [12]

Kain's case shows how the tide of suspect's rights keeps rising. A new body of law is now developing on the question, "Must I blow?" Even after the right to a lawyer has been fully met, this rich vein of Charter defences is still turning up gold. Parliament should screw up its Constitutional courage, using the "notwithstanding clause" to ward off Charter challenge, and make it clear that a peace officer's "reasonable belief" – not a judge's afterthought – ought to justify a demand for a breath test.

The so-called "notwithstanding clause" of the Charter (Section 33) allows our elected representatives to have their say when they think courts are making more law than sense. Parliament or a legislature may declare that the Charter does not apply to an enacted law, for renewable five-year periods. (They cannot, however, override basic political or common-law liberties, such as voting rights, free speech, fair trials, *habeas corpus* and so forth.)

The whole sorry situation has driven provincial legislatures to take away from the Court as much road-safety enforcement as they can. If a peace officer in Ontario is "satisfied" that a driver is impaired, he may summarily lift his licence for 90 days. In B.C., an officer can impound the car of a driver who refuses to be tested. The officer's discretion is subject only to administrative appeal.[13]

These measures may well save lives, but they are far more oppressive of due process and civil liberties than anything Therens suffered. Whether they survive Charter challenge remains to be seen.

What infuriates me about the *Therens* case – and the demon brood it spawned and continues to spawn – is the way that facts, as well-established as they can be, are deep-sixed in the courts. Therens, if we are to believe his arresting officers, had been impaired, as charged. He knew it, everyone knew it – including the judges. And yet turning a blind eye to the truth has come to be the normal way to conduct a criminal trial.

Just think what this is doing to criminal procedure – leading courts into one dense briar patch after another while wasting prodigious amounts of time and money. And not for any benefit to victims, society or even – in Therens's case – the accused himself. His neighbours hardly thought better of him because of his acquittal. How could such a ruling act as a deterrent? And think of the example his acquittal holds up to other drivers, many of whom are a good deal more blameworthy and dangerous than he.

Some time ago in Vancouver, a driver, stoned on alcohol and drugs, sped through a red light and killed a young woman, Tara Nash. The driver had a long record of drunk driving convictions, in addition to tickets, licence suspensions and jail terms. Tara's grieving family and her fiancé are left with a numbing ache that will never quite go away.

Would anyone in his or her right mind make it harder, not easier, to get a killer off the road? Or place stumbling blocks in the way of peace officers checking for unlicenced drivers? According to recent statistics, some four percent of B.C. drivers are unlicensed. Yet they are unlikely to be stopped unless caught committing some vehicular offence or at a rare roadblock. How can we sit and watch as legal barricades are erected to prevent facts from being brought to light? This state of affairs only impugns the reputation of the justice system.

The Honourable Antonio Lamer, Chief Justice of Canada, had this to say in one of his judgements:

"The public may not understand that the Charter is there to protect the accused from public opinion."

Excuse me? Could Canada's Chief Justice be suggesting that we protect accused persons by excluding credible and relevant evidence? With all due respect, I can't help feeling there is something patronizing in this statement. Ordinary, informed and conscientious citizens can have good, even better, ideas about advancing civil liberties in the public interest.

Peace Officers Found Guilty of Diligence

In 1986, Chief Justice Lamer led his Court in rejecting an eloquent, passionate and sensible dissenting opinion of Mr. Justice Zuber of the Ontario Court of Appeal. Three young men had been seen drinking beer in the garden of the house next door to that of Mark Laframboise and his wife. When the couple went out, shutting their dog in their garage, one of the beer-drinkers called out, "Do you always put your dog in the garage when you're away?" The Laframboises said they did.

The next evening at about 10 p.m. the threesome was back in the garden when the Laframboises went out again. No prizes for guessing what happened next. Their house was broken into and a stereo, some liquor and other items stolen. Both the victims and a neighbour drew the attending officers' attention to the three young men next door. They were found and escorted into the cruiser. An officer told them, "You guys can save me the trouble of coming back by telling me where the stereo is." One took him up on the offer, leading the officer to a crawl space under a house where the stereo was stashed. Fingerprints of all three men matched those found on a rear window at the Laframboise home, as well as those on the stolen goods. All three admitted their guilt.

An open-and-shut case? Only to you and me, it would seem. To the Ontario Appeal Court, the situation was far more elaborate.[14] It decided, two to one, that the culprits had been "arbitrarily arrested" when the officers were trying to see whether they were responsible, and if so, whether there was evidence to charge them. That was Charter Breach No. 1.

Charter Breach No. 2 was that the trio should have been offered a lawyer. Other mitigating factors, said the Court: the offence was not "serious" (tell that to Mr. and Mrs. Laframboise); the accused were first offenders (good grounds for lenient sentences, not acquittal); and the officers were overzealous and really had little to go on without help from the suspects.

All the evidence was eradicated. The Crown's case collapsed.

Justice Zuber, dissenting, said the officers had more than "a pure flight of fancy" to go on. Indeed, they had the intuition and experience of 20 years' service. "Yet they are now characterized as the wrong-doers," with their conduct described by the trial judge as "shocking and nefarious." (That judge really caught the Charter spirit!) In Justice Zuber's view, the officers were to be commended for carrying out their duty without any abusive coercion. He continued:

> "A person untutored in the law, but believing the primary purpose of the criminal law was the protection of the public, would find the result in this case difficult to understand…Crime detection cannot be governed by Marquis of Queensberry Rules…We must not make the price of truth too high."

Alas, Justice Zuber's voice, well worth listening to, cries out in a legal wilderness.

Canada's highest court upheld the acquittals. Only Madam Justice L'Heureux-Dubé demurred, adding to Justice Zuber's dissent that "the plight of the victims ought to have been a consideration."

You can't help admiring the justices of our high courts for their learning, their hard work, their patience, their sincerity. But they seem to undergo a sea-change as they ascend the ranks of the legal profession. Here are the words of the late, and much missed, John Sopinka, before his appointment to the Supreme Court, taken from a textbook he co-wrote:[15]

> "The essential purpose and feature of the trial system in our society is the search for the truth."

How that purpose has been lost in a high-minded but dangerous pursuit of Charter rights – rights without responsibilities! Now we Canadians appear to be in hot pursuit of American criminal justice, where "motions to suppress evidence" are the order of the day.

In a Mellower Mood

Mulling over the seeds these decisions have scattered, I think back with nostalgia to the fair number of such cases I defended in my years as a lawyer. As a sole practitioner, I took pretty much what came through the door. When someone up for impaired crossed the threshold, I'd size up the evidence and, more often than not, throw the fellow on the mercy of the court.

If he had been driving drunk and faced testimony of liquor-laden breath, an unsteady walk and so on, I'd tell him that the fine the judge would impose would be much less than the fees for a trial. Contrition, I'd advise, if it's really sincere, is always spotted by the judge. And it'll be good for you. A light fine and licence suspension will be better than you'll get trying to convince a judge you are not what you are. I suppose that today, some would want to cite me for malpractice for carrying on in this manner.

Of course, if my client insisted, I would take it to trial. In one case, a sawmill worker, Andy Good, was looking forward to his day in court. After his shift, he'd loaded up in a stripper bar until he was seeing double. Driving home, he crashed into a drugstore at an intersection, where he sat dazed at the wheel, with broken bottles, boxes and jars raining down on his vehicle.

Andy tried to tell me he had been in good care and control of his vehicle, even if some might see him as guilty of vehicular "breaking and entering." I warned him the judge would tick him off, but the stubborn fellow ignored this advice. He was sentenced to a fine, suspension and my bill, plus a lecture from the judge who allowed him not one iota of sympathy for the shock he'd suffered.

Now there is no question in my mind – and I hope none in yours – that our drunk-driving laws are seriously impaired. But spun from *Therens,* like some addled spider's web, are yet more decisions – decisions that give succour to the perpetrators of deeds much darker than driving under the influence of alcohol.

A Stick-Up Man Forgets to Clam Up

On October 26, 1982, Ron Manninen held up a Mac's Milk store in Toronto. It was just another job for Ron, who was well-known to the police. He'd have walked if he hadn't been careless – and if, at the station house, after being cautioned, his princely pride hadn't led him to make a damaging admission.

Unlike Paul Therens, Ron *was* informed by the police of his "right to retain counsel without delay." But without Ron's recklessness and conceit, there'd be no Manninen case.[16] And that would be a pity, for the case provides a front-and-centre viewing point from which to examine the flaws of Canada's criminal justice system.

First, a little background. This day, Ron had stolen a car. Later, he put on his gloves, sunglasses and a nondescript hooded sweatshirt, then chose his target. Soon he was inside the Mac's Milk store, waving his gun at some terrified employees and a customer or two. Then, scooping up the money, Ron ran to the car and drove away. Not, however, before someone jotted down the license number of the stolen vehicle.

Perhaps Ron wasn't watching enough TV cop shows, or he'd have known enough to ditch that car and steal another. After all, he thought of himself as a pro. But that touch of thoughtlessness was enough to lead the police, three days later, to both the car and Ron.

The police arrested him with their weapons drawn. To them, Ron was a dangerous character. True, he had never shot anyone, but things can easily go wrong in his line of work. An armed robber might lose his cool if an employee were too slow with the money or seemed to reach under the counter for a gun or to set off an alarm. Hold-up victims have been known to suffer far worse than just an attack of nerves that lingers for weeks.

Later, down at the lock-and-key, the sergeant read Ron his Charter caution. But Ron was feeling cocky, ready to put the law through its paces. "I ain't saying nothing till I see my lawyer," he told the officer.

Despite Ron's words, the officer continued questioning him. The first two queries were innocuous: name and address. The next was baited: "Where is the knife you used when you ripped off Mac's Milk?" This stung Ron's pride. A professional hold-up artist doesn't use a knife.

"What a lie!" he blurted. "I only had a gun in the store. The knife is in the tool box in the car."

Another officer was sent to look in Ron's car and duly returned with the knife. Now the sergeant asked the obvious question: "What do you use the knife for?"

"What the fuck do you think I use it for?" Ron spat. "Are you fucking stupid? I want my lawyer."

Although Ron was found guilty at trial, he appealed. The Supreme Court excluded Ron's confession under the "lawyers' section" of the Charter. Once he said the magic words, "I want my lawyer," the law dropped a Teflon cloak over him that fended off any embarrassing police questions. It had been a grave impropriety for the officer to have asked what he had been up to. Never mind that answering was his choice after being told he didn't have to say a word.

The police operate under a kind of Catch-22. They are duty bound to look for clues to solve crimes and round up witnesses. They should also try to question suspects – provided they do this in a civilized manner. If their questions are clever, so much the better. We go to some expense to train detectives to be at least as smart as their quarry. Often, their interviews with suspects run smoothly, caution or no caution. Innocent suspects usually want to talk, and even guilty ones sometimes talk freely in preparation for throwing themselves on the mercy of the Courts.

However, when someone like Ron is taken into custody, it's not at all likely that he'll answer questions. And if he has to confer with a lawyer before the questions are asked, you can bet he won't open up. For what will be the advice of a smart criminal defence lawyer?

> "You have the right to act like a fool and talk your head off. But talking can't help you. And not talking can't be held against you. Besides, you could spoil a good alibi you may come up with later."

Fortunately, some judges, following in the footsteps of the noble King Canute, try to hold back the rising tide of Charter-inspired defences, sadly with as little success. For instance, in 1990, Michael Carston appeared before the New Brunswick Appeal Court. He had been doing time for an earlier offence when an officer, disguised as a fellow prisoner, was slipped into his cell. Soon Carston was bragging to his new cellmate about his break-in and theft at the Red Lantern Tavern. Charged with this crime, and knowing his boasts would be used against him, Carston pleaded guilty. Shortly thereafter, he thought better of this and, after consulting a "jailhouse lawyer," he appealed. Carston argued that he'd never have bragged about his B&E if the mole had given him his Charter rights (presumably by saying, "I'm a cop, you know – you should have legal advice before mouthing off to me"). The Court, upon due consideration, wouldn't buy this and left him convicted by his own incautious words.[17]

15

Poor Carston! If only he had put off his admission of the Red Lantern job for just a few more months – until the Supreme Court really tore into jailhouse confessions in the case of *R. vs Hebert* (see Chapter 6, "Taking a Canadian Fifth"). He'd have been back at work instead of doing time.

Sometimes it seems almost as if the Law were plagued by a haunting fear that someone, somehow, somewhere, might be found out. Yes, we are getting into deep waters. Perhaps the right to silence, that pillar of our justice system (of which more later), isn't the virtue it's cracked up to be?

Consider this. The appeal court did not rule out Ron Manninen's admission because the sergeant had winkled it out of him. True, the officer had used a baited question. But the courts conceded that the police must sometimes use deception in the performance of their duties.

What police conduct, then, does or does not cast the law in such a poor light that probative evidence must be stricken from the record? Contrast the State's treatment of Therens and of Ron, with (to take one example of many) the ill-treatment it meted out to one Ralph Barnes. And be aware that this treatment was *not* held to blemish justice enough to void his conviction.[18]

Well and Truly Stung, Deceived and Trapped

One fine day, Ralph Barnes was walking along Vancouver's Granville Mall, a pedestrian strip frequented by down-and-outs, druggies and other undesirables. Barnes was a drifter, often down on his luck. Scruffily dressed and in need of a shave, he was soon accosted by an undercover cop, a woman. Here was deception. All undercover operatives are walking false pretences. Many pretend they are cons, getting their prey to think, "If this guy's crooked, I can trust him."

Acting on a hunch, the officer asked Barnes to kindly sell her a fix. Barnes refused. Again she asked him, this time with the kind of sidelong glance that seems to promise bliss. Hooked, Barnes went off and returned with what she had asked for. He was promptly busted. His privacy rights – guaranteed by the Charter but apparently not as important as the right to a lawyer – had been severely abridged.

Barnes's conviction went the distance, with his lawyer arguing that the police had been engaged in "random virtue testing." But the top court held that the law's repute did not require exclusion of the incriminating evidence.

Had I sat on the case, I would have found Barnes had a justifiable, though borderline, defence of entrapment. The officer had gone too far. Rather than simply affording him the opportunity to err, she had induced the commission of an offence that otherwise might not have occurred.

Barnes, as we have seen, had not been under arrest when he incriminated himself. Our old friend Ron, however, had been in custody (and had to be or he'd have taken off). Barnes was not afforded any constitutional rights – no warning, no access to counsel. Ron, on the other hand, had been told he needn't answer questions. The long and the short of it is that Ron was given greater protection than Barnes, who had no idea the State was about to do him in. Neither Therens nor Ron could complain of ill-treatment by the Law to the extent that Barnes could. But only Barnes was convicted. Where's the logic in that?

Jack Weisgerber, an estimable member of the B.C. Legislature in the late 1990s, was charged with hunting out of season. Until this unfortunate turn of events, Jack had been a shoo-in candidate for the prestigious job of Speaker of the House. But canny wildlife conservation officers had placed a decoy deer beside a highway, rigged up with a tiny motor to blink its eyes and twitch its body as if real. Jack and a companion saw this creation one day. Stopping the car, Jack's companion took pot shots at the decoy. Both men were charged.

Now, you might cry foul at such a ruse, which seems awfully close to entrapment. But how else can conservation officers protect wild species, understaffed as their department always is, and with seldom a witness around to testify to an offence?

Underage teens have occasionally been hired by the State to go into small corner stores and illegally buy cigarettes. The merchant – who has trouble enough getting by in competition with the sprawling supermarkets – can lose his licence for selling tobacco to minors. Yes, the ploy is underhanded, but teen smoking can cause dangerous addiction and severely damage health.

Sometimes, social necessities oblige the Law to use deception. And yet, we law-abiding citizens have to live with some of these lies, while Charter rights protect seasoned criminals. Now, which is the bigger blot on Justice's fair name?

Murder, They Wrote

Suppressing truthful evidence is the Law's flaw – sometimes, even when the evidence points to murder. James Clarkson was found sprawled in his armchair, a bullet hole in his head, a rifle nearby with no fingerprints. His wife was cautioned and offered a lawyer. "No point to that," she blurted. Distraught, intoxicated and hysterical, Mrs. Clarkson was heard to confess the killing to her aunt. Later, at the cop shop, she let slip some incriminating remarks.

The Supreme Court majority suppressed her statements, saying the police had "flagrantly" violated her rights by questioning her in such a distraught and inebriated condition. She was not in a frame of mind to be able to waive her right to counsel. To admit her statements would bring justice into disrepute, the Court opined. The woman was acquitted. [19]

But the Court had posed, and answered, the wrong questions. Dissenting, Justice William McIntyre asked himself the proper questions, rather than worrying about her rights. Did she have an operating mind? Know what she was saying? Grasp the consequences? He still rejected her admissions as insufficiently trustworthy to prove her a murderer beyond a reasonable doubt.

Wesley Evans was another confessor of murder, but the Court excluded his confession because of an alleged infringement of the suspect's rights. Evans was in custody, suspected of the brutal killings of two women in Matsqui, B.C., one with 25 stab wounds, the later victim with her throat slashed. Of subnormal intelligence, this 30-year-old man was said to be "functioning at the level of a 14-year-old child." Chatting to an undercover officer in his cell, Evans first admitted to one killing, then to the second. At one point, he talked of killing again.

The Court found that allowing the testimony of a mentally deficient suspect would sully Justice. Evans was cleared. But if his were true confessions, as they seemed to be, most thoughtful people would want justice to act upon them. Mrs. Clarkson, after a domestic tragedy, was not likely to re-offend. But Evans himself said that he was. The hard question – what to do in the way of custodial prevention and treatment for a man who had suffered a childhood brain injury – was left unanswered.

Legend has it that Justice Mary Southin, then a B.C. trial judge, after being obliged to exclude key Crown's evidence in one case because of a procedural transgression in its acquisition, asked the prosecutor if he had anything more to say. "Bring me a blindfold and a cigarette," he replied. Southin rejoined, "Sorry, no smoking in the courtroom."

A Charter for All Reasons

Do we really need a Charter? It was put in place to protect individuals from unjust, abusive and overbearing coercion by State officials. But it must be user-friendly to victims, actual and potential, and to the public interest, as well as to suspects. This it can be, without turning a blind eye upon relevant and reliable facts and statements. Unfortunately, as Peter Burns, a dean at the University of B.C.'s law school, wrote:

> "Since the advent of the Charter, our Courts have become engrossed by procedural issues instead of substance." [20]

To this we can add, borrowing from Shakespeare's Sonnet 110, that the law has come "to look on truth askance and strangely." Truth, meanwhile, is caught in a legal maze, with escape difficult and sometimes impossible.

The Examination

Before closing this chapter, I'm going to set a pop quiz. Mark your own papers — I trust you.

1. Stauros Tzimos, who spoke no English, landed in Canada with some rolls of counterfeit money. A Greek translator Chartered him, explaining he had the right to see a lawyer. Stauros didn't want a lawyer. Nevertheless, a local Ontario judge felt that "he seemed to be reaching out for help" and "he did not seem to understand our Charter." (Not a surprise; few judges can make head or tail of it.) Even though Stauros's fake money was confiscated, the evidence was ruled out, and he was acquitted without ever being examined on his knowledge. [21]

   In 500 words, describe in detail your opinion of this judge's opinion.

2. Neil Corbett was arrested for robbing a store, Chartered and questioned. But detectives then went on to question him about a more serious bank robbery without once more advising him of his rights. Neil talked himself into having done the bank job. Although he really had done it, his confession was ruled out. [22]

19

In 1,000 words, describe your reactions upon hearing this tale, and give your opinion on the judge's sagacity.

3. Joe Esposito stole a credit card and used it at the gas station where he worked. Detectives questioned him at his home, without lawyering him. Joe admitted making out the sales slips. He was arrested and then lawyered. The Court ruled that Joe "had not been 'detained'" in his own home; it ruled his admission in.

   In 500 words, detained in your own home, attempt to explain the logic behind this ruling.

4. Guy Robert had beaten, sexually assaulted and murdered a young woman. His admission, plus his video reenactment of the crime and the fact that he led officers to where he'd thrown the victim's wallet, were all excluded under the "lawyers' section" of the Charter. The Court stated this evidence was "derivative" and the "fruit of the poisoned tree" of a Charter breach. The Court granted Guy a new trial to determine whether a jury could consider the wallet evidence.[23]

   In 500 words, explain whether, if you were a juror on the re-trial, you would consider the wallet story helpful or unhelpful in your job.

6. Justice Zuber has asked, "Are we making the price of truth too high?"

   In 500 words, answer his question, referring to the above cases.

Chapter 2

Trial Judge Hawg-Tied
by Motorcycle Gang

*"Let the public but once perceive that [the Law's] grand
principle is to make business for itself at their expense,
and surely they will cease to grumble."*

– Charles Dickens

Courts bog down when they don't get on with the job at hand, which is ascertaining the truth. In *Bleak House,* Charles Dickens satirized the mid-19th-century English Court of Chancery, with its interminable delays, costs and empty legalisms, its classy barristers from Temple Bar and its mousy solicitors and their overbearing and underbred hangers-on. As this great novelist saw it, Chancery was devoted to the principle that a good estate should not be frittered away on its beneficiaries. He struck the nail soundly on the head when he wrote:

> "The one great principle of the English Law is to make business
> for itself. Viewed in this light, it becomes a coherent system, and
> not the monstrous maze the laity are apt to think it is."

Legal affairs have not changed that much since Dickens's time, as the modern-day case of the Iron Hawgs makes clear. The Hawgs ultimately succeeded in putting the trial judge himself in the dock, at least figuratively. Whatever may be said of this sort of proceeding as Law, and plenty is said, it has little or nothing to do with Justice.

First a word about these Hawgs. An Ontario bikers' gang, the Hawgs were into more than riding in formation and collecting toys for needy children at Christmas. Their real work concerned narcotics. Specializing in cocaine, LSD and methamphetamines, the Hawgs marketed their products all over southern Ontario. (A peace treaty with a rival gang, the Outlaws, had averted some of the nasty casualties of turf wars.) Their cross-border exports probably contributed mightily to Canada's balance of trade, although the figures didn't show up in government records.

Of course, the Hawgs' products ravaged the lives of thousands and crowded hospitals and jails. In order to pay their bills, their customers often turned to crime – hold-ups, B&Es, forgeries and so on. Often, the bikers' girlfriends, who'd acquired a taste for their lovers' merchandise, were forced into prostitution to come up with the necessary funds. Even the Hawgs themselves were at risk, for the gang expected absolute loyalty. A Hawg suspected of less than this could find his body dumped far from the clubhouse, sent off to meet his Maker without benefit of clergy.

A War to Lose

Here I wish to pause and indulge myself in a brief rant. You may, if you wish, skip this distressing portion, which contains my thoughts on a modern plague: narcotics. Of course, these chemical compounds go back a long way in human history. Coca, from which cocaine and heroin are derived, was and still is a staple crop in the Amazon River basin. But today, drugs are a malignant disease in our society.

There is no denying we are now losing the so-called war on drugs. They have infiltrated our schoolyards, with susceptible teens attracted by their forbidden allure, as some are to alcohol and tobacco. They have penetrated commercial sports, glamourized by hockey players, basketball stars and others. They are advertised in magazines like *Hemp Times* and considered a necessary part of life in fashionable social circles. They offer a holiday from hopelessness on inner-city streets, as well as overdose deaths and needles infected with HIV and hepatitis C.

We try to stanch their penetration through our porous borders, but without much luck. Of the thousands of containers that pile up continuously on our ocean docks each day, very few can be laboriously and randomly searched, unless there's a tip-off. Add to this the millions of law-abiding automobile and airplane travellers among whom drug smugglers can mix in, and we've got a big problem. Meanwhile, powerful and dangerous synthetic substitutes can be mixed in home bathtubs from acetone and other store-bought chemicals. Home-grown marijuana is becoming one of B.C.'s biggest cash crops and a major export item.

Forty-odd years ago, a puff on a marijuana cigarette led directly to jail – if you were caught – plus a possessions count for whoever gave you the toke. This is no longer the case, which is perhaps just as well. Court dockets, already bursting at the seams with the million charges laid in Canada each year, can't cope with this sort of thing. Nor are there many vacancies in our hoosegows.

So today, purveyors of dope, if picked up, merely get fines, being careful to have only small quantities on them. They stash their supplies in bushes or trash cans, with look-outs stationed to watch for lawmen or thieves. As for the high-rollers who make the big bucks, you'll find them – if you find them at all – in pricey condos, behind surveillance cameras and triple-locked doors. If they possess any product, which is unlikely, they'll have time to flush it down the toilet. To them, it's strictly business. As our laws now stand, they are untouchable. As the tribulations which beset the Iron Hawgs trial show, attempting to exact retribution through the courts is a waste of everybody's time and money – defence lawyers excepted.

Instead, I suggest we should decriminalize "soft" drugs and place them under firm provincial control. Turn some of the profit into public coffers, as we do with alcohol, and take profit out of the criminal market, although we'll never get it all.

But in addition, we must build treatment centres for addicts who want to be cured. For those who don't, there is no use wasting money. Addicts who like their "highs" more than reality will not stop until they've bottomed out in misery. Alcoholic Anonymous members know this. AA won't enroll people until they are determined to give up drinking.

For the hard-core junkies, let's give them methadone or shots by prescription at unglamorous clinics – but within limits. What narcotics do to brain cells, to neural fibres, no one can really calculate. These substances are an international problem, and we don't want to become a haven for users from all over the world.

We can, and should, spend as much time and money on taking customers away from the criminal marketplace as we do going after suppliers. And we need to forget about our privacy fetishes and, to increase consumer protection, insist on more urine and other tests, taken randomly.

Above all, change those laws that hamper, if not abort, the detection and punishment of traffickers. If need be, we can use the Charter's "notwithstanding" section.

Back to the Hawgs

With that out of my system, let's return to the convoluted case of the Iron Hawgs. For years, the Ontario Provincial Police, notorious for their suspicious nature, had kept an eye on the Hawgs' comings and goings. Tip-offs (although not admissible as courtroom evidence) had arrived via the underworld grapevine. In 1983, the OPP began surveillance in earnest. As a way of keeping their quarry firmly in mind, they called the operation Project Boar.

The police took their suspicions and observations, detailed in lengthy affidavits, before Judge Scott of Ontario's Supreme Court. In an *in camera* hearing, the police asked leave to eavesdrop on the Hawgs' telephone conversations. Judge Scott, exercising judicial discretion, agreed. Countless tedious and costly hours of listening followed, as the tapes were painstakingly transcribed.

On January 22, 1985, with enough goods on the gang to satisfy the prosecutors, the police raided the Hawgs' nine fortified clubhouses and arrested 80 suspects there and on the streets.

On May 11, 1987, the trial got underway, like a slow movie reeling backwards. Before any real legal business could proceed, the presiding judge, Judge O'Connor, was first asked to entertain eight preliminary objections from a battery of defence lawyers. He agreed, as the law requires. After three months of hearing these objections (with the jury excused), the judge ordered the trial to begin. However, one objection would turn out to contain enough live ammunition to eventually sway the minds of a majority on the Supreme Court of Canada.

The verdicts came down in July of 1988. Some Hawgs were convicted and some acquitted. Some, of course, had copped guilty pleas in exchange for leniency. The guilty were sentenced. But the Hawgs' lawyers, not satisfied, decided to launch an appeal.

In May of 1992, by two to one, the Ontario Court of Appeal affirmed the convictions.[1] One of the majority, however, Mr. Justice Finlayson, was moved to expostulate. Surveying these proceedings, and perhaps having breakfasted on salted oatmeal, he wrote:

> "Unless we, as courts, can find some method of rescuing our criminal trial process from the almost Dickensian procedural morass that it is now bogged down in, the public will lose faith in our adversarial system of justice. As Jonathan Swift might have said, we are presently sacrificing justice on the shrine of process."

Now what did the Learned Judge mean by "justice"? Perhaps he, like I, viewed justice as a process to seek the closest approximation of the truth, while of course providing opportunity for the accused to make full answer and defence to the case presented against them. This the Hawgs had in the lower court. Truth appeared to have won out.

One of the appellants, Durette, had been unable to make bail following his conviction because of other unrelated run-ins with the Law. So by the time his appeal was heard, this unfortunate Hawg had already served the required jail time of his nine-year sentence and graciously abandoned his appeal. Had he not, the Court of Appeal, like the White Queen in Alice in Wonderland, would have been forced to decree: "Sentence first, verdict after!"

Then, on March 17, 1994, the Supreme Court of Canada – by four judges to three – overturned the Hawgs' convictions [see *R v Farinacci et al.,* 1994, SCC 88 CCC (3rd)]. The Crown was virtually forced to start all over again. What had finally found a target? Simply this: Judge O'Connor was held to be in error in "over-editing" the affidavits on which Judge Scott based his decision to allow the phone taps. In vain did Judge O'Connor explain that he had suppressed parts of those affidavits to protect sensitive police surveillance methods, not to mention the identity of informers. The Supreme Court held that he had been overzealous and had cut out too much. The big question – had the Hawgs committed the crimes with which they were charged? – fell by the wayside.

Madame Justice L'Heureux-Dubé vigorously led the dissent. This appeal, she said, concerned "judge-made laws." In other words, it wasn't the Charter that made us do it. She pointed out that the affidavits, even as edited, amply justified the phone taps. And she noted that defence lawyers had cross-examined, for nine full days, three officers who'd sworn the affidavits, and they had examined two undercover officers (in the process blowing their covers) for three full days. Anything, she wrote, that might have let the bikers infer the identity of informers would be dangerous to the informers' health, since dead men tell no tales. And, as I hardly need point out, unmasking informers hardly encourages others to come forward and assist other investigations.

Yet, in all the forest of words in the judgements at all levels, there is an eerie silence as to what should *not* have been culled from the affidavits. No rational suggestions were made as to how words expunged from the documents might have assisted the Hawgs in making full answer and defence to their actions. Substance had become immaterial.

Which leads us to the inevitable question: Is it sensible to reward the accused with new trials just because a judge erred in preliminary proceedings relating to the gathering of evidence?

Perhaps you will count yourself lucky not to have been empanelled to serve on the Hawgs' jury. You did not have to swear to "true deliverance made between our Sovereign Lady, the Queen and the prisoners at the Bar," nor were you irritated to find yourself excluded for long periods from the courtroom while lawyers debated what you could and could not hear. You, the bastion of our liberties, no more prone to err than the "experts" who pronounce the law – and much better at truth-finding than a lie detector – would *you* have let the words from *The Gospel According to John* flit through your head: "The truth shall make you free"? Would you have steeled yourself for yet "another objection, Your Lordship"? Or would you have concocted medical reasons to escape jury duty?

The Chief Justice of Canada, the Honorable Antonio Lamer, was among those who set aside the Hawgs' convictions. On January 14, 1995, addressing the Empire Club, he said:

> "Some trials are so long, one wonders whether the process will not collapse under its own weight. We must find a way to

retain fair process with practical results in a reasonable time and at reasonable expense."[2]

Now, no one can quarrel with that exclamation by the learned Chief Justice. But had he forgotten his Hawgs' case? That case did seem to be something of an echo of Prodigal's Law: "Process expands to fill the time and money available."

Has process ceased to expand? Not likely. The Court allowed the Crown to start all over again with a re-trial of the Hawgs, whose convictions had been lifted. That, however, is easier said than done, even forgetting time and money. The memories of witnesses fade as time goes by. Some may have taken off for parts unknown; others taken leave of this Earth. Still others could have second thoughts about testifying against the Hawgs. And who's to say that some the Hawgs, on bail pending appeal, might not skip? Of course, it was game over anyway for those accused who had pleaded guilty, betting on a lesser rap.

Some fond souls may be thinking that cases like the Iron Hawgs only come along once in a blue moon. Not so. Consider, if you will, the distressing spectacle of what has come to be known as the "Just Desserts" murder case – after the location of the crime, not, unfortunately, after the triumph of Justice.

In April 1994, four men with dark complexions were caught on security videotape as they burst into a trendy Toronto restaurant. Robbery was on their minds; the tragic shotgun shooting death of a restaurant patron was soon on their hands. Four years later, Ontario justice Brian Trafford had faced a flurry of motions, appeals, legal skirmishing, nit-picking, blocking tactics and various other assaults on the justice system brought by more than 50 lawyers representing the accused, at a running total legal aid bill already in excess of $2 million. Most recently, counsel for the accused dared to bring up the court's delay as a reason why charges against their clients ought to be dropped.

In denying this request, an exasperated Mr. Justice Trafford ruled that "the delay in bringing this case to trial is largely explained by the relentless efforts of defence counsel…to scrutinize and attack every component of the administration of justice." In a rare and admirable display of candour, he wrote in November 1998: "While defence counsel have, on occasion, said the accused want a speedy trial, the actions of the defence counsel show that a speedy trial is, in reality, the last thing the accused want in this case."

In another case reported in November 1998, a B.C. man accused of milking the federal Scientific Research Tax Credit program was acquitted – after a *400* day trial – when the judge ruled that his income tax returns were inadmissible due to the way the Crown obtained them. The Crown is appealing.

The Charter Is Held Up at the Border

Law enforcement officers of every species have had their daily work hamstrung by complexities borne from the Charter. Consider the dilemmas faced by Customs officers, constrained by precedents such as the following.

Blaine, Washington, August 1992. A pleasant couple, the Rodenbushes, arrived at Canada Customs, declared a gift of clothing for their children and compliantly paid $70 in duty. But wait – things are not always as they seem.

Mr. Rodenbush worked for a lumber company in Duncan, B.C. The company's principal had asked Rodenbush and his wife to drive to Seattle and bring back two suitcases. These they would obtain in a hotel from one Chris Hauser. The trouble was, Hauser was under surveillance by American law-enforcers. They alerted Canada Customs that the pick-up had been made.

At the border, an inspector asked to search the Rodenbushes' car. They were asked to wait in an interview room. The inspector, noticing scratch marks on the inside of the suitcases, found in the lining 4.2 kilos of cocaine, 76 percent in purity, worth $1.6 million on the street. A superintendent asked the inspector to question the Rodenbushes. When he did so, they told him an obvious lie, saying the suitcases had been purchased in Nanaimo and had not been out of the car. This lie appeared to incriminate them. They were arrested and read their rights.

The trial judge convicted them. But at the appeal, the judge said the Rodenbushes had not had what he was pleased to call "the guidance of the *Therens* case," which had just come down. The convictions were upset and a new trial ordered, with the incriminating lie ruled inadmissible. This left the couple room to substitute a better story. The appeal court judgement held that the Rodenbushes had been "detained," as determined under the Charter, that they had not been given a lawyer or a caution before revealing their secret, and that the Customs officer had "deliberately flouted the Charter rights of the accused." Thus, the incriminating evidence had to be buried.[3]

The court had nothing to say about the probative value of the evidence. It was just a question of what, Charter in hand, might be considered to be "fair" treatment of the accused.

This case has left Customs officers in a quandary. They must draw insidious distinctions between "innocent" and "fairly innocent" travellers and darkly criminal ones. Consider the following scenarios:

- A couple without contraband, not even a pack of cigarettes, nervous perhaps, is "detained" for a search of luggage and car, even of their persons. Should they view this as just one of life's misadventures, to be put up with bravely?

- A inward-bound traveller is found to possess two bottles of California wine, purchased, he says, in Canada. However, there are no Liquor Board labels on the bottles. "Come on, where did you buy them?" the officer queries. The traveller ends up paying double duty plus the Liquor Board mark-up. All in an officer's daily work.

- A pair of tourists arrives in a car which, upon inspection, contains something really dangerous – guns or drugs. Now our poor officer is in deep Charter waters. He or she must be extremely careful with the questions. These characters might trip themselves up, and the courts wouldn't like that!

Here's another case to ponder. On March 13, 1997, a bad actor flew into Toronto's Pearson International Airport from Switzerland. He'd bought his ticket the day of the flight, he was jumpy and he refused to meet the Customs officer's eye. He held a Ghanaian passport but admitted he had never been to Ghana. A luggage search revealed some undeclared liquor. He denied any criminal record, but the computer showed assault and incest. He was "detained," Chartered and escorted to the drug toilet facility. He spoke twice by phone to a lawyer. A strip-search came up empty. He refused a urine sample, but at length, nature called and his pee tested positive for heroin. Four hours passed – longer even than most passengers must look for lost luggage – and our man finally excreted "bodily wastes," along with 84 pellets of heroin. At this point he admitted all. Convicted, he appealed. By two to one the Ontario Appeals Court freed him.

Why? The "detention" was too long. The "search" was all right by the *Customs Act* ("reasonably suspicious"), but not up to Charter snuff ("probable grounds"). His defecation was "conscripted." All evidence was thrown out.[4]

Madam Justice Karen Weiller, dissenting, thought otherwise. She took the word of the experienced Customs officer who thought that here was a "good prospect of a drug swallowing." She considered that demanding a urine sample was "a minimal interference with bodily integrity"; that the subject was the cause of his own prolonged detention; that border searches, "to protect the public," should not be held to stringent legal tests.

What does it say about our judicial system that so many of the most eminently sensible judgements are uttered in dissent?

In December 1998 the Crown appealed to the High Court. How will it go? Toss a coin!

Here we have a great example of the sporting theory of justice – horses and hounds in the morning. Don't spoil the hunt by not giving the fox a chance to get away. Such precedents result in a big increase in the numbers of plea bargains, some of which work out quite well, while others give our justice system a black eye.

Pleading Down for a Discount Sentence

A band-aid solution to the interminable delays and complications imposed in part by Charter-generated arguing, the plea bargain has come to be, in recent years, a huge and inescapable part of our criminal justice system. As caseloads bulge and complexity proliferates, disposing of charges through negotiated settlements becomes more necessary than ever. Thus it is that about 80 percent of all charges laid in Canada are settled with guilty pleas in exchange for leniency. This is the oil that prevents the wheels of justice from grinding to a halt. Without it, armies of judges would have to be appointed, acres of courtrooms built.

Not that there's all that much wrong about the usual plea bargain, freely arrived at and subject, as it ought to be, to judicial scrutiny and approval in open court. On a charge of shoplifting, for instance, Crown and defence lawyers try to work something out. How strong is the Crown's case? The defence's? Has the accused a record? What led to the offence? It could have been a bout of treatable kleptomania, a thoughtless act of desperation or mere avarice. Will a lighter sentence or probation bring a sinner closer to repentance? Or is this a hardened, persistent malefactor who has calculated discount sentences into the cost of doing business? The latter would call for a trial and effective deterrence.

Fortunately, all snitches don't get discounts. One man, charged jointly with his 18-year-old wife in the murder of a hitchhiker, offered the prosecutor, "I'll roll over on my wife, if you'll let me down easy." This daring, but questionable, proposition was turned down.[5] (Its impact on his marriage has not been reported.)

All this proliferation of pleading leaves a lot of responsibility in the hands of Crown Attorneys. They have to exercise discretion in a fair and open process, with the Attorney-Generals subject to final accountability when complaints are brought. Too often, the A-Gs slough it off, saying, 'This is the advice I received from my department, or from a special prosecutor.' Do they think we don't know that it's up to them to accept or reject advice?

There is something seriously wrong with bargaining when the Crown has to buy the testimony of one guilty soul in order to convict others. In such circumstances the quality of justice is strained indeed.

Evidence for Sale

Karla Homolka was a partner in crime with her husband, Paul Bernardo. From 1989 to 1993, these two committed a horrific series of rapes and murders that shocked Canadians from coast to coast. The Ontario prosecutors felt, especially in light of the technicalities of investigations and trials, that they needed Homolka's evidence to ensure the conviction of Bernardo. So she was able to sell her testimony for a price that included a reduced sentence of just 12 years. A judge approved the sale. To make matters worse, he did so in closed court, fondly believing that possible jurors in the later Bernardo trial would deliberate better without knowing of the formal plea-bargaining proceedings. Not that the judge could prevent jurors from the influence of rapidly spreading rumours and gossip. To make matters still worse, the judge did not require Homolka to be examined on oath about her participation in all of the rapes, some 18 in number. This was presumably in deference to the misguided idea that any compelled interrogation might be considered a violation of civil liberties. Unfortunately, although predictably, this led to a growing public perception of injustice, once Homolka's culpability in the crimes subsequently came to light.

Inequality Under the Law

Consider as a cautionary tale the short, unlucky life of Allan Dodds.[6] He capped his life by serving up to the Ontario Court of Appeal a most unsavoury plea bargain.

As a young teen in Montreal, Allan used to go joy-riding in stolen cars. Tucked away in detention for this predilection, he studied guns under his criminal peers, learned how to use a drill to obliterate registration numbers and how to shave gun barrels to confuse ballistic experts. After graduation, he embarked on his career as an accomplished robber with violence. By his late 20s, Allan's long-playing record included doing time for a restaurant bombing, not really his preferred line of work.

In 1988, facing more charges and tiring of prison life, Allan decided to squeal on one of his tutors, Richard Pizzardi. An aerial photographer, Pizzardi allegedly scouted good robbery targets as a sideline. Leaving the robbery and violence to others, so it was alleged, he contented himself with a slice of the proceeds.

Allan approached Pizzardi to ask for some gainful employment, or so Allan later testified. Instead, Pizzardi lent him $200 and then told him about a gay man who lived alone and collected gold coins. "This would be a really easy hit," the older man suggested. With no further prompting, Allan broke in on the loner, beat him up and made off with some $3,400.

Facing this and other charges, Allan traded his testimony against Pizzardi for total immunity, $3,000 in cash and a hideaway under the Witness Protection Program. Pizzardi was convicted and appealed.

But before the appeal could be heard, Allan had a change of heart. Secluded in his hideaway, he missed his old business associates. He recanted his testimony against Pizzardi in a sworn affidavit, even offering to take a lie-detector test to prove he wasn't lying when he lied about not lying. With the appeal still to be heard, Allan − back in business − was shot dead in a bungled Montreal robbery.

When the appeal rolled around, Pizzardi's lawyers touted the Charter's equality section, Section 15. How even-handed was the justice system that had given the far guiltier Allan special and generous treatment? You guessed it. The Court allowed that the late Allan Dodds was "an unsavoury character" and "unworthy of credit," dead or alive. But, holding its nose and swallowing hard, it refused to free Pizzardi and sent him back for re-trial.

There will always be times when such plea bargains are necessary to catch criminals who hatch clandestine conspiracies. Still, if the Law were not sinking into what our oatmeal-eater, Judge Finlayson, called a "Dickensian procedural morass," there'd be fewer odious deals for courts to digest, not to mention fewer dubious informers for juries to disbelieve and fewer thugs-turned-squealers hiding out at public expense in overcrowded protection programs.

But just so you don't despair completely over the collective IQ of our judiciary, here's a sensible nugget, once more from Justice Mary Southin of the B.C. Court of Appeal. She is reputed to have invented the following riddle:

Q: What's a narcotics case without a Charter argument?

A: A plea of guilty (or at least a plea bargain).[7]

Some Questions to Stump a Law Student

Allow me to set you an exam, based on what we have discussed in this chapter. You have one hour. Neatness counts! Any giggles or signs of shock and dismay, however understandable, will result in a score of nil.

1. The accused was still unconscious after being rushed to Vancouver General Hospital from the scene of his car crash when a doctor, for medical reasons, drew a vial of his blood. A policeman, for his own reasons, asked the doctor for some blood and received it. Its analysis revealed the accused's insobriety. But the High Court couldn't hear of this, ruling the blood had been "conscripted" by the State from a non-consenting citizen. (Bear in mind that blood found on a driver's seat cushion, however loath the driver was to part with it, can be proof of impairment.)[8]

   Set out your views on conscription.

2. The accused was pulled in for petty theft and duly cautioned. He persisted, however, in volunteering a whole string of his crimes, hoping to court favour with the officers. The trial judge held that he should have been re-

Chartered from time to time in his "free flowing colloquy" (or at least told to shut up). But the appeal judges said no; "that although the Charter violation was a serious one," the Law's repute required his loquacity to count against him.[9]

Question: Shouldn't some people hold their tongues and appear to be honest, rather than blathering away and removing all doubt?

3. The accused, seen to drive in a zigzag fashion and stop for a green light, was pulled over at 1 a.m. in Ville D'Anjou, Quebec, given right to counsel and so on. The officer, suspecting inebriation, asked him to recite the alphabet and do some physical coordination tests – touch his toes, pick up some coins, walk a straight line and so on. He failed all but was acquitted by the Appeal Court because his lawyer had not come to review and critique his performance.[10]

Question: Is drama criticism a legitimate extension of the right to counsel?

4. One Mr. Shallow walked into the private parking lot adjoining the police station to relieve himself. He was arrested for trespassing. Searched incident to his arrest, Shallow was acquitted of carrying cocaine on his person. His lawyer, Mr. Goose, successfully argued the arrest was unlawful.[11]

Question: Which do *you* find more objectionable: his arrest or his acquittal?

Now, hand in your papers, and leave the room quickly. Your papers will not be graded, but your ability to stomach absurdity in the legal system will.

Chapter 3

The Law's Delay[1]

"I call on the judicial and legal professions
to declare war on courtroom delays."[2]

– Hon. Antonio Lamer

This stirring call to arms, issued in the spring of 1995 by the Honourable Chief Justice of Canada, could not have been more timely. An ever-expanding spider's web of legal complexities is paralyzing our criminal justice system. Drawn-out hearings, bursting caseloads and burgeoning costs are the order of the day. In five years, from 1989 to 1994, the cost of Canadian law enforcement rose by $347 million. The taxpayers' bill reached a staggering $10 billion in 1994, and shows no signs of diminishing. Over that same period, the cost of criminal legal aid doubled to $603 million, and policing costs rose by 30 percent.[3] Add in the burgeoning private security industry and ask yourself, have we benefitted by an increase in public safety?

In vain do governments throw more money into the system to build more courtrooms, appoint more judges and prosecutors and construct more prisons. The greedy monster only demands more, putting on weight as it lumbers along without picking up speed.

Meanwhile, the cause of courtroom delays is in plain view in the court-rooms themselves – a preoccupation with legalistic lacunae that has nothing to do with either fair process or the determination of guilt or innocence. Process thickens as it comes to a boil.

An Ancient Malady

In *Hamlet,* the Prince of Denmark ranks "the Law's Delay" as a misfortune on a par with "the pangs of disprized love." Much earlier, in 1215, King John's barons raised the same complaint. Confronting the King, arrayed in arms, they made him concede in the Magna Carta that "to no one will we deny, to no one delay – justice or right." Those barons knew that they did not want to languish in the King's dungeon on some trumped up charge without a day in court, let alone an early one, just because the King wanted to lay his hands on their lands, their wives or their gold.

In 1982, this right made its way into our Charter in Section 11 (b): "Any person charged with an offence…has the right to be tried within a reasonable time."

Sharp eyes will notice that our Charter section does not confer rights upon the victims of crime, only upon the offenders. That is a step backward from the Magna Carta, which stated that "no one should have to put up with slow justice, neither the person on trial, nor the one he injured and anxious to have justice redress his wrong."

How have the courts made this Charter right available? Not, unfortunately, by attacking the procedural causes of delay, but by attacking their symptoms. The courts afford relief in three ways, as I will explain.

The Askov Cure

The Supreme Court spelled out this "solution" after one Elijah Askov waited for almost three years to have his day in court. It dismissed the charges against him (*R v Askov,* 1991, SCC 74 DLR (4th) 355).

There is some justice in that. People arrested and awaiting trial live with pre-trial anxieties and want to clear their names, if they can. Still, we must not fall too far for the romantic notion spoken of by Supreme Court Justice Cory, who talked of the "exquisite agony" of accused persons, as if they could hardly wait to hear from judge or jury. Most malefactors, especially if they are out on bail, want anything but an early trial, hoping something will turn up, that witnesses will die or their memories fade or that they can make some money in the interim – often in the trade that got them into the trouble – to pay for the best defence money can buy. They are not anxiously waiting to hear the cell door slam.

The results of the Askov remedy did not live up to its intentions. After that decision came down, prosecutors in Ontario alone crossed 47,000 pending cases off the court calendars. Most were petty offences, to be sure, but many were grave crimes. The same results followed in lesser numbers in other provinces.

Today, cases are still being chopped off clogged court lists. On April 28, 1998, according a report in *The Vancouver Sun,* Chief Justice Robert Metzger of B.C.'s Provincial Court appealed to the Attorney-General to give him five more judges. "Criminal cases," he said, "are delayed to the point where we risk dismissal of thousands of charges." This despite the efforts of prosecutors who, trying to cut backlogs, simply don't lay a lot of charges which should, but never will, come to court.

Here we have a cure every bit as bad as the disease.

In *Askov,* the highest court failed to discuss the apparently undiscussable: the complex rules of criminal evidence. Nor did it enjoin the judge to penalize dilatory players.

Thus, two years after Askov's case was dismissed, a woman alleged that she had been raped on a poolroom table by a Toronto bartender. Five times she and the bartender showed up for trial, ready to roll. Five times it was no go. No courtroom was available, no judge to sit, jurors were tied up in other trials. After two years of this, the bartender was given a discharge he hadn't earned. As for the complainant, she went home lamenting that she had received less than even-handed justice.[4]

In 1994, a teacher in a Mayne Island, B.C., school was charged with sexual assault upon a 16-year-old girl. She had come to the home of her former teacher to make a little money babysitting. Another girl also complained of his molestations. He had, however, awaited trial for nearly 18 months, without either him or his lawyer abetting the delay. In 1997, the B.C. Court of Appeal tossed out all charges against him (*R v Cocker,* 1997, 89, BCAC 276 (App Cases)).

The girl's father thought the decision brought the administration of justice into disrepute. He lamented to the newspapers that "the delays were just as hard on the innocent victims as on the perpetrator, but he got all the benefits. They bared their souls in court and were brutalized by the system."

The Jack Attack

Of course, all this devouring time spent on trials, motions, appeals and re-trials is Charter-exempt, whatever the "exquisite agonies" the defendant suffers in its passage. However, one Andrew Jack, a Nova Scotian, created a notable exception – for all our rules have the odd exception or two.

In 1988, Jack was charged with the murder of his wife. To this day, her body has not been found. In 1990, after a month-long trial, a jury convicted him. Appealing, Jack won a second trial because of "inappropriate comments made by the judge to his jury." The charges were reduced to manslaughter, and this time he was acquitted – only to have the Appeal Court order a third trial in which a jury convicted him of manslaughter. Jack appealed again, winning a fourth trial on grounds that the trial judge too heatedly "exhorted" the jury, which was having trouble making up its mind.

One appeal judge, however, Madam Justice Helper, would have entered a stay, saying that the accused, in jail for 14 months and "subject to multiple proceedings," should not have to endure a fourth trial. That, she said, "would tarnish the integrity of the Court."

In 1997, when the case went on to the Supreme Court, it first ordered a fourth trial, but then, agreeing with Justice Helper, nixed it. This raises a question: did Jack's case die of old age in its legal bed (not under the Charter's "Delay" section, but under Sec. 7, "Fundamental Justice")? [*R v Jack*, 1997, 117 CCC (3rd) 43(SCC)].

In passing, allow me to reflect, inappropriately perhaps, on "cruel and unusual punishment," as outlawed in Section 12 of the Charter. European courts refuse to order extradition to the United States of accused murderers who could end up on Death Row. Many sentenced to death in the States await their fate for years. One, in 1998, was 38 when he was finally electrocuted for a crime he committed when he was but a lad of 17. That, in itself, is unacceptable in justice, and European judges won't participate.

Pre-Charge Delay

Once upon a time, time limits applied to charges in criminal cases, murder excepted. Now they are pretty well gone. So some wait in fear for an old crime to surface, while others, to their surprise, find themselves before the Court. Take the case of Mrs. McDonnell, of Nova Scotia, who thought her ordeal long over. In 1982, she and her former husband were charged with the death of a child in their care. The charge was dropped for lack of evidence.

But 33 years later, her estranged son turned Crown witness, saying the child had not died from a fall from a fence but at Mrs. McDonnell's hand. She was re-charged, this time with non-capital murder. Her lawyer professed she could not get a fair trial. Her former husband was dead; so was the neurosurgeon who did the autopsy. The constable's notes were missing, as was the inquest transcript. The Supreme Court agreed, and the second charge was dropped (*R v MacDonnell,* 1997, 114 CCC (3rd) 145 (SCC)). Criminal justice had lost its prey. But had it not, would the courts have tried the same person who had allegedly done the deed? Or someone else, quite different perhaps, after 30-odd years?

Our laws' delays are taking on weight, fattening volumes on library shelves. "Specialists" in delaying tactics are emerging as a sub-species of the Criminal Bar. A recent random sampling of criminal lawyers in Ontario identified quite a number who claimed to specialize in this arcane field. And more than a few others said they were not averse to using such tactics for the benefit of their clients.

Does not such an attitude among these sworn officers of the Court bring justice into more "disrepute" than some trivial Charter breach?

Russian Cokes: The Pause that Failed to Refresh

Sometimes, justice delayed can prove lethal to the accused themselves. That was the situation in the "Russian Coke" caper, which went to trial in Vancouver in early 1990. On February 17, 1992, after 28 months, the case against the conspirators was terminated without ever reaching trial.

Like his co-conspirators, Eugene Alekseev had been able to make bail after his arrest. And like the others, he had been overheard by the authorities conducting drug deals on the phone. Why should he have pined for speedy justice? The guiltless want it, but Eugene hardly fit that profile.

The Learned Judge threw out this case, first and foremost because of the Charter's stipulation for a speedy trial. But underlying his action was the knowledge that the ranks of the accused were thinning alarmingly.

The cocaine conspirators, dubbed the Cokes, were Russian-born – the Brothers Alekseev and the Brothers Filanov, assisted by various friends and relations. They had burst onto Greater Vancouver's narcotics market in 1986, armed with automatic weapons. Not fastidious in their use of either firearms or muscle-power, this motley crew consisted of feisty 20-somethings with a spot of Russian gangland experience under their belts.

However, the Cokes' entry into the market was not welcomed by the city's established drug traders, especially the Hell's Angels. The Hell's Angels are a rough but exclusive bunch. They won't take in "blacks, snitches, cops or hypes" (junkies can't be trusted not to rat); nor can members retire for "personal reasons." Once, a Mr. Ozolin tried to bow out of the organization, only to get shot, along with his girlfriend – gaining not only early but permanent retirement. The Angels' annoyance grew when the Cokes, at gunpoint, relieved a group of them of $200,000 worth of quality cocaine.

Now, no one nixes fallen Angels without retribution. First, they gunned down Serge Filanov, free on bail and quietly going about his business outside an East Broadway motorcycle shop. Not content with that, the Angels then kidnapped Taras Filanov, holding him for ransom for their highjacked cocaine. The ransom was paid, but Taras's body was nonetheless found shortly thereafter in a wooded area near the University of British Columbia, his hands handcuffed behind his back, his face blasted by a shotgun.

Next, another Coke began to miss his court appearances. Few doubted that, as a 1950s *film noir* would have it, he was "sleeping with the fishes." By this point, three of the Cokes had had their cases summarily transferred to a higher supernatural jurisdiction. There, no doubt, their punishment will fit their crimes.

Eventually, all the disappeared turned up in the station house Unsolved Murders file. Any witnesses to their deaths piously resisted testifying against the Angels.

You can't help but wonder whether the departed Cokes might have been better off in jail awaiting trial. However, the Law does not count risk of death as just cause to deny bail, although the Charter does, in Section 5 (11), guarantee the right "not to be denied bail without just cause."

But clever Eugene Alekseev outlived the case and made the Law Reports. He had attained the great age of 20 before his body was found in a Mexico City hotel, where he'd checked in as Eric Anderson. The Mexican police classified his death as a suicide. But his girlfriend had just been arrested in California. She'd been carrying 18 kilos of cocaine to Vancouver. You can rest assured that Eugene, a take-on-the-world, iron-pumping type, did not end his own life.

What took the Cokes' trial so long to get started? Preliminary bouts ate up 28 months and prevented the main match from ever reaching the court. These included:

- A "restoration motion." Right off the bat, the brothers (perhaps motivated by their legal aid lawyers) sought the $24,000 or so in cash found on their persons at arrest.

- A motion for "interception of private communications; review of authorization." When it came to phone calls, the brothers had been less than discreet.

- A "judicial inquiry into the behaviour of the police and the press." The brothers' lawyers suspected that someone in the police had tipped the press, thereby besmirching the accused by association with unsavoury underground characters. On this issue, the defence team subpoenaed three officers and two reporters, subjecting them each to cross-examination by eight different lawyers.

But the *coup de grâce* to the Crown's case was still to come. Staying all charges, the Judge ruled:

> "The information was laid in September 1989. But the accused Alekseev was not arrested until February 1990. In November 1989, his co-accused in his absence waived their Charter right to speedy trial. The fact that the agreement was made with the best of intentions and in the hope it would reduce the overall cost in time and money, could not justify the removal of this accused's rights in his absence and without his knowledge and consent."[5]

The Court had been unwilling to say that a man on the lam from the police had forfeited his right to speedy trial. Eugene walked free, leaving the courtroom with his caring parents, a happier man but a lonelier one, en route to his final destination in Mexico City. And Taras Filanov, the one found on the UBC Endowment Lands with his face blown off? Charges against him for possession of an Uzi submachinegun had been stayed at the request of police, lest they interfere with drug charges that were later stayed by the federal Crown.

Beaulac Helps Himself to Extra Justice Helpings

Jacques Beaulac knew how to put criminal justice through its paces. In 1995, he left Quebec to live in B.C. There he piled up a two-page record for such misbehaviour as impaired driving, forgeries, theft and aggravated assaults. "All petty offences," as Jacques saw it. To his murder judge, he claimed he got his legal training "at the knees of jail." This tutelege included "jailhouse lawyers" doing time with him, his own courtroom dramas and advice from the Legal Aid lawyers he would dismiss as not up to scratch. Jacques even fired my friend Mike Rhodes, his first murder defender, telling the Court that "he was an idiot."

It was Mike Rhodes (known around Court as "Endless Rhodes," for the thoroughness of his cross-examinations) who told me how the Mounties got this man for murder, a tale my credulous ears could hardly believe. Mike tries to "Rumpole" me occasionally, and I particularly recall a story about his prostitute client who was up for sentencing in a New Westminster courtroom at 10:00 a.m. She was late, and the judge was furious. Mike looked out of the window, heard the click-click of high heels from the parking lot, and saw his client busily stealing hub caps from late-model cars.

But his Beaulac story, improbable as it was, was all true. I checked it later as the law reports on his murder saga came out.

In 1982, the body of a 21-year-old woman had been accidentally found in Lynn Creek, in a remote backwoods area of North Vancouver. She had been severely beaten, though the autopsy gave drowning as the final cause of death, and was identified as Mary Anne Costin. The RCMP had nothing to go on until 1989, when his own brother, in Sherbrooke, Quebec, cast suspicion on Beaulac.

The Mounties immediately assigned a Quebecois officer, Staff Sergeant

Pineault, to strike up a friendship with their quarry, masquerading as a gangster and wearing a wire. It was a canny ruse if there ever was one. Conversing in French, Pineault boasted of his biker-gang connections in the East, and the easy money they brought him. Beaulac wanted to join, only to be told that "just anyone can't be a member – you have to establish credentials, character. What have you done to prove they can trust you?"

"I killed a woman in North Vancouver seven years ago," Beaulac told him, walking right into the trap. But that wasn't good enough for Pineault. "Oh, I can't just take your word for that. Can you prove it?" says he.

So off went Beaulac, taking Pineault to the Vancouver Public Library where they looked up old newspaper clippings, confirming the details Beaulac had put on tape. He was arrested, and the long court saga got underway.

From 1990 to 1997, Beaulac went through three preliminary trials, two appeals, several applications to the Supreme Court, motions of all kinds and the final trial. He tried to pin the killing on someone by the name of Norris, a "crazy drunken Indian" with whom he and the deceased had supposedly been drinking, snorting and having sex. But this trial was aborted by the judge after a month and a half. The wife of a juror had overheard some words that passed between Rhodes and the accused. What could have been said that the jury shouldn't know? The law keeps too much hidden from juries, when it should just trust citizens to get it right.

The second trial was upset on appeal. The trial judge had mistakenly described the defence of drunkenness in long-established terms. But this defence had been widening, and is still widening, under the Charter. The fine distinctions might bother second-year law students, but not jurors. They will excuse, or not excuse, a defendant for drinking, or reduce murder to manslaughter on their own appreciation of the case, and of the accused – but rarely on nit-picking legal distinctions.

Through it all, over seven years, Beaulac kept playing his French card. He disdained an interpreter at his first trial, saying he wanted to "talk direct to the jurors." At the second, he used a court interpreter, but impugned him for not grasping his East End Montreal patois. Then he raised the ante, demanding an all-French third trial and a French-speaking judge. Not only that, but all the people from whom the jury would be picked would have to be francophones, as well as the lawyers, reporters, clerks and sheriffs – everyone except witnesses speaking through an interpreter. This was a tall order in B.C.

Tall, and spurious. For five years in B.C., Beaulac had done business in English. He had lived for two years with a woman who spoke only English, and he had never asked for an interpreter either at his first trial or at any of his previous criminal trials. He had addressed countless judges in English with passion, if not eloquence. His murder conviction stuck in the B.C. Court of Appeal (see *R v Beaulac,* 1998, 120 CCC (3rd) 17).

But stay tuned. The case still limps on. I asked Mike Rhodes about his old client and he told me in October 1998 that the books were under preparation for another appeal visit to the Supreme Court of Canada. Perhaps Beaulac will some day be free at last from those annoying courts.

The object of justice is the prevention and cure of crime at the least cost to individuals and society. But what of the costs, in dollars and time, of *l'affaire Beaulac?* Justice's resources are not bottomless. We know that, far down in the system, apprehended children at risk are waiting months, even years, for hearings to determine who will be their guardians and care-givers, and how safe their futures will be. What does delay cost then? What are the resources spent on them, for judges, social workers, hearings and treatment? The answer: never enough.

If time was a wastrel for Beaulac, it was a dodge for Andre Kollen. In his case, as we shall see, the Crown took a fall for delaying the disclosure of a tipster, who, in any event, had no trial evidence to give.

Public Stung in Dutch Sting

Andre Kollen of Amsterdam was a liar and a thief. He also boasted first-hand acquaintance with the drug business, being himself a trafficker. In May 1989, he decided, for his own ulterior reasons, to help the police nail a big-money international narcotics cartel. Andre apparently yearned to get on the right side of the authorities for a change. Besides, he wanted to make some money. So he told the Dutch police, who told the RCMP, about a group of druggies who bought hashish in Vancouver and sold it, at a mark-up, in Europe and across Canada. He also helped them orchestrate a sting. His price? A mere $40,000 in Canadian dollars, cash.

All went merrily. Five ring leaders arrived at the Vancouver Airport Hotel, where they flashed one million dollars in cash to RCMP undercover officers, proving their financial responsibility. In turn, the RCMP undercovers gave them a one-kilo sample of quality hash to test for potency. Later, in an upstairs room, one million in cash was passed to the undercovers in exchange for 2,000 kilos of hash, to be delivered in the parking lot. The five were arrested, caught red-handed.

The trial began in B.C. Supreme Court on January 27, 1992 and expired on September 21, 1994. The defence team exhibited an understandable desire to have Kollen share the spotlight with their clients. The Law offered its assistance, steadily distancing itself from the crime. Not a word of guidance was ever to be heard on whether the accused were guilty as charged.

The defence team argued that its clients had been entrapped by the police. This wouldn't fly because they had been in the drug business for some time. The also laid the fey charge that the RCMP had themselves trafficked in narcotics by providing the sample kilo of hash. This almost flew, but in the end reason prevailed. (The sample, by the way, was never recovered.)

Eventually, an improbable debate reached the Appeal Court.[6] The defence wanted to see the legal advice that the RCMP had received to show "lack of good faith" on their part. In truth, good advice or bad, the RCMP were simply, doggedly, trying to get their men in the midst of a legal minefield.

Finally came the fatal delay. The defence wanted Kollen out of the shadows to be grilled. The Dutch government and the RCMP balked at this, saying Kollen had neither witnessed anything done by the accused, nor said anything to them, nor heard them say anything. Both authorities further stated that, if Kollen were exposed, they would not proffer their assistance. However, they eventually gave in, and Kollen was produced in Amsterdam. The judge, the lawyers and a court stenographer were flown over to take testimony.

Alas, they had waited too long. Months after this, the judge ruled that the Crown's failure to disclose Kollen sooner was "non-disclosure resulting in delay." This had breached the accused's "right to be tried in a reasonable time," and he dismissed all the charges. A year later, his reasons for judgement came down. The Crown, considering the state of the Law, did not appeal the acquittals.[7]

When, then, can the defence counsel pluck off an informant's cloak of anonymity? The law, needless to say, is never quite settled on this or other points of criminal evidence. It unfolds, as if faithful to the maxim of the late Nicolai Lenin. The Charter steps forward, then takes one step back, two steps ahead and so on, as we shall see in the following saga.

Crime Stoppers Anonymous

In 1995, a Crime Stopper passed by the Vancouver home of Richard Liepert. Crime Stoppers are sterling citizens who combat crime by keeping a look-out for the police, volunteers who sometimes get a cash tip for their tips. In this case, our Crime Stopper was interested to see just how did Liepert's garden grow – with inter-planted marijuana all in a row.

So, enter the lawmen. They have their own look-see; they lay their charge. They neither need nor want to call their Crime Stopper as a witness. It's hard enough getting such heroes to volunteer without exposing them to unwanted limelight – or worse, harassment or harm. At trial, the defence moved to see the Crime Stopper's report. The judge allowed this with some editing, blackening out any clues to the good citizen's identity. There, in a lucid moment, the Court decreed that official Crime Stoppers could stay in the shadows, as long as the "innocence of the accused is not at stake."

A good though short step back! But why not a long step back to the old commonsensical rule. Courts need not kill time by fussing about witnesses neither the prosecution nor the defence want to call.

Surprise Breeds Delay

This brings us to the subject of disclosure rules. The Crown should, as it did in the Kollen case, disclose in a timely manner to the defence all of its notes of evidence bearing on the commission of the crime. Fairness demands this; the defence should know the case it has to meet. But while the Crown must disclose all, the defence need disclose nothing. Instead, it can lie in the weeds and tailor its reply to what it knows of the Crown's evidence – or even manufacture alibis based on weak points in that evidence. This "right" of the defence to surprise the prosecution is another prescription for longer, costlier trials.

One-sided disclosure works this way, with sexual assault cases a particular example. A rape charge is laid. The defence lawyers pore over notes of statements the police have gathered from any possible witnesses – including, of course, the complainant. Moreover, the defence can, if a judge finds this relevant to the complainant's credibility, go over notes of any psychiatric interviews she may have had, or any counselling at a rape crisis centre. The accused, meanwhile, need say nothing until, at trial, the prosecution closes its case. Then the defence comes out with its side – "It wasn't me" or "It was me but I was drunk or robotic" or "She said I could." What should be an even-handed search for truth becomes a trial by ambush.

Is help on the way? In 1992, Supreme Court Justice Sopinka wrote: "The suggestion that disclosure should be reciprocal may deserve further considera-tion by the Court in the future."[8] Without, I hope, too much delay. Meanwhile, the Court is still taking one-sided disclosure well beyond the lunatic fringe. This is what it did to one woman who complained of sexual abuse.

She had gone to a women's centre in Windsor, Ontario, complaining that she had been sexually assaulted years earlier by her teacher when she was his grade seven and eight student. The social worker made some notes and told her to take her story to the police. She did so the next day, and the Crown charged her former teacher with gross indecency.

At trial the defence lawyer demanded to have the notes taken at the women's centre, for any help they might be in cross-examining her. But to preserve confidentiality, the centre, as a policy, shredded such notes. This it could lawfully do, prior to any subpoena to produce them. The defence still had the notes of what the woman told the police, as well as a statement made by her husband and her brother.

But the High Court made the missing notes the centrepiece of the case. Since they were absent, they stayed the charge, by a five to four decision.

The minority justices considered these to be flimsy grounds to avoid judging the case. They pointed out: that there was only a "possibility" the notes might have affected the verdict; that the notes had never been in the Crown's possession; that the accused was entitled to a "fair" trial, not a "per-fect" one; that witnesses sometimes die or disappear, but that in itself does not abort a trial.

As for the victim, if her story was true, she suffered far, far less than per-fect justice.[9]

Why is the "right" to keep the prosecution guessing still revered in Canada? Why, when reciprocal disclosure is becoming acceptable in England and Wales, and even in California? Because our practice is protected by such weighty canons as:

- The accused has no obligation to assist the prosecution. (With a better atti-tude, the accused might not have found himself in trouble in the first place.)

- The accused who must disclose his defence is violating his rights against self-incrimination, a.k.a. the much-vaunted "right to silence."

But both these "rights" are illegitimate and unfair. There are after all two sides, not one, in criminal cases. One is the accused, the other the Queen or Crown. Or, as the Americans put it, "the People." The Queen, the Crown and the People all have a value to protect — the checking of criminal activity. That's a value equal to the accused's rights to make full answers and to be let off if not proved guilty beyond a reasonable doubt.

One-sided disclosure violates Section 15 of the Charter, which says "everyone" is entitled to equal treatment before and under the Law. Where's the equality when a rape victim has to reveal all relevant evidence right off the bat, while her alleged tormentors don't have to?

A Prescription for Doctored Testimony

A guilty soul wants to take his time with his story, and does so if he has smarts. He doesn't want one that bumps right into strong Crown evidence. Instead, he seeks one that finds a way around it. He wants time to find an alibi, one that can't be easily shredded by Crown witnesses. He wants a story that jibes with what friends or accomplices may be able to say on his behalf. He wants rehearsals of his testimony with his defence counsel. All this, I'm sad to say, is an incentive to fabricate. If someone can rob or rape, he can lie.

What is illiberal, in serious cases, about all important witnesses giving statements under oath before a Justice of the Peace in an orderly setting, as soon after the event as possible? It surely would shorten court proceedings, and the resulting statements would be more believable to judges and jurors. Memories would be fresher; there'd be less concocting. If this offends an accused's right not to be "conscripted," well, maybe that right has feet of clay, as we will see later in Chapter 6.

Delay Marches On

I draw this chapter to a close with two tales. One is horrendous, but both tell us more than we want to know.

Tale No. 1

In 1996, six defendants stood trial in Vancouver for two alleged gangland-style slayings. They were all acquitted after nine months of trial. The Crown appealed, chiefly because it came to light that one of the accused had slept with a juror, during the course of the nine-month-long trial. (Better at all odds than sleeping with the fishes?) The six defence counsel asked the Court of Appeal to order the Attorney-General to pay them $300/hour, equal to what he is paying the Crown Counsel (and more than the $175/hour his two juniors get). The appeal is estimated to last for six weeks. Then, perhaps a pre-trial, another appeal…Do "billable hours" stretch out cases? Yes, they do.

This headline appeared in the *Vancouver Sun,* December 18, 1997): "Four Lawyers Reject $858,000 to Handle Appeal of Alleged Killers." What goes through the mind of an ordinary Canadian, when he or she reads that?

Tale No. 2

This harrowing story cost Ontario Legal Aid much less. I am indebted for it to Judy Stead, an informant whose cover I hereby blow. It concerns a caring mother with children, and a disabled girl, adopted as an infant. Diagnosed as mentally retarded, with fetal alcohol syndrome, she was enrolled in her teens in a special class. At 17, in the schoolyard, she was chased, tackled and sexually assaulted by three boys. A passing stranger saw her being attacked, half naked on the ground. One of the boys confessed and implicated the other two; the stranger also testified. Each boy had a lawyer. The case took two court years. All three were convicted.

The trial involved numerous Charter motions, "a lot of them utterly irrelevant," according to the prosecutor. Fifty, repeat 50, distressing court appearances by mother and daughter. The mother called the ordeal an "emotional nightmare," and reported jeers and jostling of the victim in the halls by the boys and their friends, resulting in lasting traumatic damage to the girl. The mother indicted a justice system that, she said, "rewards lawyers for delaying cases." Once again, process had eaten substance.

Canada's judges have a special responsibility to keep trials on track toward truth and even-handed justice. They should oversee a pre-trial process in which prosecution and defence exchange information bearing on the innocence or guilt of the accused. At such a get-together, the merits of the charges could be discussed, with some perhaps dropped and disposed of in return for guilty pleas. In exchange, a more lenient sentence might be handed down than if guilt were found after a lengthy trial. This might also result in lawyers being better prepared for trial of the issues in dispute, with less inconvenience to jurors and witnesses.

Judges can arrest a drift toward the Fox-and-Hounds Theory of Justice. Below the border, the judge is simply an umpire, keeping the players to the rules of the game, deciding on objections, while the two sides fight it out. U.S. judges cannot even comment on the evidence, which Canadian judges can do to assist juries in their deliberations – fortunately for us. But unfortunately – no doubt the fault of Charter jitters and fears of reversible errors on appeal – our judges too often shy away from cutting short the tedious and often repetitious cross-examination of witnesses. Sometimes whole batteries of lawyers go at it, well-versed in techniques to cleverly confound the truth.

The upshot is that too many trials are not getting beyond the *hors d'oeuvres* to the main course, with social costs to pay: in time and money wasted, in guilty offenders acquitted and in major criminal conspiracies virtually immunized. But there is a still greater cost: diminished public respect for the criminal courts, which citizens rightly expect to serve the simple end of truth and fairness.

Would we but hearken to the words of Madam Justice Beverley McLachlin:

> "Perfection in justice is as chimeric as perfection in any other social agency. What the law demands is not perfect justice, but fundamentally fair justice…A system which is workable, affordable and expeditious…not diverting from the true issues." [10]

An Easy Exam This Time

To accommodate readers who by this time may have reasonable and probable grounds to admit to some confusion, I am setting an open-book exam that can be completed at home, no time limit.

1. The province of Ontario engages a mole on a contingency-fee arrangement to infiltrate a criminal ring. He is to receive the full $100,000 only if he gets the goods from the conspirators. The court, though concerned

that he may have listened to the tempter and thrown in some lies, accepts his testimony.[11]

Question: If you had acted for the province, would you have hired this mole on contingency fees or on billable hours?

2. A gun fanatic and collector of my acquaintance, rumoured to hunt with an automatic weapon and chafing at the restricted weapons law, takes an assault weapon to a Vancouver police station. He wants to be charged so he can then Charter-challenge the law. The desk sergeant thanks him for coming in, confiscates the weapon and says, to this fellow's chagrin, "There will be no charges."

Question: Was this "process" too short, or just right?

3. A young man picked up for breaking and entering, with a handgun, a balaclava and a Hallowe'en mask in his possession, is charged and told by an officer that "it will be better for you in court if you tell the truth." He does, but the judge strikes out the truth, saying he had been "induced."[12]

Question: Should the officer be disciplined for telling him to speak the truth?

4. An officer on stake-out sees a shadowy figure picking up a bag of drugs. He flees, chased by the officer, who loses his fleet-footed fugitive. However, the officer's sniffing dog continues the pursuit, cornering the accused, but minus the bag. The court admits the dog's evidence that the accused was the man who made the pick-up.[13]

Question: Would you have accepted the evidence of a dog?

Chapter 4

Stepping on Parliament's Toes

*"The proper role of the judiciary is one of interpreting
and applying the laws, not making them."*
— Madam Justice Sandra Day O'Connor,
   United States Supreme Court

When Justice O'Connor made this statement, she was simply expressing what any wise person knows: True democracy requires a separation of powers, with an impermeable boundary dividing the work of elected politicians from that assigned to the judiciary. On one side of this boundary, politicians assess social problems, deliberate and pass remedial laws. On the other, judges determine the intent and purpose of the laws and adjudicate. Each side has its distinct and proper role to play, with no cross-dressing allowed.

The Constitution is offended (not to mention the press) when politicians do so much as phone a judge about a pending case. Yet judges who dally with the laws created by our elected representatives, applying them not as they are written but as they would like them to be, commit an equally grievous constitutional wrong.

Were Madam Justice O'Connor ever to peer northward from her perch and take an interest in Canadian jurisprudence, she would be shocked at the lack of prudence amongst our judiciary. Oh yes, her fine words are paid lip service in the administration of this country's criminal justice system. But too often they are honoured in the breach. She would have noticed, too, much rustling of parliamentary powers by the Supreme Court, with more ill effects than good – only to be expected when courts respond to a social question with a legal answer. She would see the Charter rights of accused persons propped up to extraordinary heights, inconsistent with the expressed will of Parliament.

Here we will see how these rights are used to clamp down on the powers of legislatures, with negative consequences to society. And we will see these rights applied, with fine legalistic reasoning, to produce results that generally curtail our civil liberties, that do not serve the public interest nor even, in the long run, enhance the welfare of many of those on trial, for whose protection the rights were designed.

Straining credulity, but gleaned from actual judgements, we will see:

- how a perfectly good criminal law was struck down because of the name Parliament gave to the crime;

- how a rape victim was further stressed by having to testify at a second trial, though justice was done at the first;

- how the rights of persons on trial came to allow judges to tell Parliament how judicial salaries should be fixed;

- how a "legal" decision threw Canada's refugee admission procedures into turmoil and abetted criminal activities;

- how the invention of the defence of "non-insane automatism" plunged judges into debating whether drunkenness could be a defence to a charge of drunk driving;

- how a jury was left in the dark about the bloody shirt found on a murder suspect.

What has been Parliament's reaction as slices have been cut from its constitutional loaf? Our elected leaders, awed by the Court, accept the erosion of their powers without protest, and without invoking Parliament's own right to re-enact good laws, notwithstanding judicial Charter rulings. Alas, the Parliamentary dogs do not bark.

You Can't Call that Murder!

Yvan Vaillancourt of Montreal was an armed robber by trade. In 1981, he and his partner in crime, Yvon, burst into a billiard room with the intention of relieving the patrons of their valuables. Vaillancourt was armed only with a knife; his partner, who had a gun, got into a struggle with one of the patrons and shot the fellow dead. He then fled, never to be found. Vaillancourt, however, was arrested and charged with what is known in Section 213 of the Criminal Code as "constructive" murder – in other words, being a partner in a violent crime when you should have known someone could be killed.

His defence, with which he regaled the jury, went like this. "Yvon and I planned the hold-up, sitting in a *brasserie*. I told him he could take his gun only if it wasn't loaded – because I had a bad experience in another robbery when my gun accidentally went off. So Yvon removed three bullets from his gun and gave them to me. I put them in my glove and went to the toilet to smoke a joint. Then we set off for the pool hall."

During this tale, which may have been a tall one, Vaillancourt was asked to identify his glove, which had been found in the pool hall. He did, and three bullets fell out, giving the jurors a nasty turn. They had no trouble convicting him of constructive murder.

Vaillancourt, however, appealed. After striking out at the Quebec Court of Appeal, he went on to the Supreme Court, where his lawyer attacked the Code's constructive murder section, which states:

> "Culpable homicide is murder…where a person committing a robbery…with death ensuing…carries a weapon…whether or not he means to kill anyone or knew death was likely to occur."

On the face of it, his lawyer hadn't a leg to stand on. After all, Vaillancourt had brandished a knife. He should have known a death was a distinct probability. He was manifestly engaged in a violent crime that endangered human life. This, Parliament had defined as a crime. It had the ring of fundamental justice about it. Nevertheless, Vaillancourt's legalistic hotshot did get a leg-up from the High Court. Saying Section 213 (D) was "of no force or effect," it awarded a new trial.[1]

There, Vaillancourt's lawyer argued that, with the word "murder" in the section, a judge could get carried away and stick an accused with a stiffer sentence than his part in the crime warranted. "Murder" calls for an automatic life sentence, with no chance of parole for 25 years (if first-degree murder) or 10 years (if second-degree). (Of course, it may not be long before these lengthy minimum sentences are struck down as "cruel and unusual punishment" [Charter Section 12]).

The second prong of the lawyer's attack was that a conviction for a form of "murder" would tarnish Vaillancourt's reputation among right-thinking members of society.

This was enough to sway the Court majority, which agreed, holding that "the stigma that attaches to a conviction for murder is extreme." Of course, the Court did not take into account that the so-called "stigma" would hardly have hurt Vaillancourt's standing in jail, where he was going anyway. Although it's true, when the knave was eventually released into polite society, he could well have lost some social standing if found guilty of murder, "constructive" or not.

But common sense, a commodity in very short supply these days, should indicate that the degree of Vaillancourt's participation in the pool-room killing should have been addressed by the sentence. In reality, Vaillancourt's jail time could have been as long as his partner's, had the partner ever been tracked down. He was much more than a look-out to a hold-up, and he may well have masterminded this job. We may also wonder if he refused to rat on his runaway accomplice.

Just for the sake of argument, let's look at the maligned Section 213. Were we to take out the word "murder," what remains is the presumably acceptable offence of being a party in a common design to premeditated violence. As Justice William McIntyre, a dissenter, pointed out:

> "The principal complaint is not that he has been convicted of a serious crime of violence, but simply that Parliament should have chosen to call it 'murder.'"

Madam Justice L'Heureux-Dubé, also in dissent, expressed a view shared by many, calling the ruling "an egregious example of misplaced compassion."

Sensible, but alas, in vain. The Court majority was telling Parliament, to paraphrase Humpty Dumpty in *Alice Through the Looking Glass:*

> "When you use a word, it means what we choose it to mean; neither more nor less. It's simply a question of who is to be master, that's all."

Never mind that forcible rape causing unintentional death is considered murder in California, with nary a constitutional challenge. And in Michigan, reckless drunkenness causing death while driving is also considered murder.

While the Vaillancourt case itself didn't count for much – the fellow went down on re-trial to conviction for armed robbery, with a sentence that took everything into consideration – it did clog already congested courts. And it did start the criminal justice system on the road to Hades. From unmaking one law to ignoring another was an easy step.

A Miscarriage of Justice

It gets worse. The High Court has also ridden right over Parliament's ordained direction, set out in Section 686 of the Criminal Code, on how appeals should be handled. This section falls under federal power over criminal procedures. If it had been followed, there would have been no need for a re-trial of the assault complaint I am about to outline for you.

On September 22, 1990, in Halifax, a 15-year-old girl was waiting in the lobby of an apartment building for a ride home. She had finished her babysitting stint for the evening. Suddenly, as she later testified, two Asian men appeared and forcibly kissed and fondled her.

The young woman laid a charge of sexual assault. In her formal complaint to the police, this girl said that one of her assailants was "fat" and "clean-shaven." Three weeks later, she picked out a Vietnamese male's picture in a photo line-up, and the man, named Tran, was arrested.

One year later, when the case came to trial, Tran turned up sporting a moustache. He had also lost a few pounds. Nevertheless, the girl again identified him as one of her attackers.

Chief Judge Palmeter was presiding without a jury. He appointed a Vietnamese interpreter for Tran, whose grasp of English was deemed insufficient. As the trial was drawing to a close, Tran's lawyer called the interpreter as a defence witness. The interpreter testified that he had met Tran casually about a year earlier, and that he then appeared to be only about five pounds heavier. His evidence, given in English, was later summarized in Vietnamese. The judge accepted the complainant's evidence of identification and found Tran guilty.

Now comes the kicker. The defence lawyer had raised no objection during the trial to the summarized translation of the interpreter's brief testimony. After all, this was a witness for the defence. However, the objection was later raised in the Nova Scotia Court of Appeal, and Section 14 of the Charter was cited:

"A party or a witness... who does not understand or speak the language in which the proceedings are being conducted, or who is deaf, has the right to the assistance of an interpreter."

The three appeal judges were not impressed. Justice J. A. Freeman delivered their reasons:

"There is no doubt that Tran was entitled to a full translation and not mere summaries. However, the impugned evidence was of minor probative value. No affidavit has been filed suggesting that Tran was not aware of the gist of the evidence elicited by his own lawyer. No objection to this presentation was made... The trial judge accepted the identification evidence of the complainant. It was not contradicted."

Tran did better in the Supreme Court of Canada, which set aside his conviction and directed a re-trial. This was bad news for the complainant. Years of waiting have a way of keeping alive fears and anxieties. Now she would have to re-live in her second testimony a painful episode in her life.

The Supreme Court's reasons, given by the Chief Justice, run to 34 pages. Although not as long as some, it is still a far cry from the monumental judgements of Chief Justice Oliver Wendell Holmes of the U.S. Supreme Court, who said he wrote his opinions in longhand standing at a high desk, ensuring they would be short and to the point. The Supreme Court's judgement contrasts with those of the Appeal Court in more than length. Justice Freeman's words seem infused with a kindly, though tough and shrewd, appreciation of human beings and their frailties, how they act and present themselves to others. But the Supreme Court judgement appears to emanate from a world remote from the concerns of everyday life, a world of learned academics and sheltered intellectuals.

The thrust of the Supreme Court judgement is revealed in these quotes:

"The Court should not engage in speculation as to whether or not the lapse in interpretation made any difference to the outcome of the case...

"No person should be subject to a Kafkaesque trial...

"An accused need not demonstrate any actual prejudice; that he or she was in fact impeded in his or her ability to make full answer and defence."

Here the Court is saying – and this does take some swallowing – that any breach of that Charter right, large or small, means that the accused has been denied fundamental justice. This is reminiscent of the abstract reasoning of medieval scholastic philosophers, who would deduce from "A" that "B" must be so, never mind whether, in reality, "B" was so or not. Indeed, the way the Court zeroed in on a literal – though not consequential – Charter breach brings to mind the old legal saw: "A judge untethered by the text [of the Law] is a dangerous instrument." But is not a judge too firmly tethered equally dangerous?

Surely the intention of those who wrote the Charter's Interpretation section had been slighted. Now the Court went on to slight the intention of Parliament. A longstanding and sensible section of the Criminal Code (Section 686) directed appeal courts to ignore technical breaches if "no substantial miscarriage of justice had occurred."

So why was this section not used to affirm Tran's conviction? No court found that any miscarriage of justice had occurred, let alone a substantial one. If justice had miscarried, it was in the denial of fair play to the victim. But all the Supreme Court said about Section 686 was, "We must not go to the curative provisions of the Code."

Well, why not? The Court's action was hardly likely to encourage appeal courts to use this section in cases to come. Our Parliament, within living memory, has passed some bad laws, but Section 686 was not one of them. It makes sense in a world where perfection in the administration of justice will always be just out of reach.

Laws passed by parliaments originate in the concerns, interests and desires expressed by individuals and groups. Their wishes percolate up through politicians into parliamentary committees, where they are commented upon by experts and others and their social and economic ramifications are explored. They are then debated by MPs answerable to their constituents.

But laws made by judges, no matter how learned and well-intentioned, do not endure this rigorous procedure. Judges must not be held accountable to parliaments, public opinion or the clamour of single-issue lobbyists. They are given security of employment until retirement in order to support this judicial independence. Doing this, however, we endow judges – especially those of the highest court – with a heady power. Their decisions can all too easily slip beyond their purview – and beyond the bounds of common sense.

The late Hugo Black of the U.S. Supreme Court once said of himself and his colleagues that "Power corrupts." [2] He was not suggesting that they might take something under the table. He meant they should be careful not to trespass on the domain of elected representatives.

So what, in practicality, was the result of the *Tran* decision? For the accused, little or no good. On any re-trial, he will likely be convicted once more, since there was nothing really wrong with his first trial.

As for the young woman, she will suffer more stress and anxiety. As for other sexual-assault victims, seeing her fate, they may decide not to make formal assault complaints. Too many women already feel, rightly or wrongly, that the justice system will treat them with suspicion rather than compassion. In the vast United States, it is estimated that a rape occurs every five minutes. But the vast majority – 84 percent – go unreported. And only two percent of the perpetrators do prison time. [3]

We Canadians may well have a better record in law enforcement. However good it is, it can and must be improved. All witnessing is burdensome, especially so for victims of crime. But without witnesses coming forward out of a sense of civic duty, the whole criminal justice system faces collapse. Judgements such as that of our Supreme Court in the *Tran* case do little to encourage them to do so.

In the *Tran* case, the Court slighted the law-making domain of the people's elected representatives, with the Chief Justice saying dismissively that, "as a matter of law, a violation of the translation section of the Charter precludes a consideration" of Section 686. Now what was the genesis of this "as a matter of law"? It appeared like a naked newborn – never mind that Parliament is supposed to be autonomous in this field. Section 91/27 of our 1867 Constitution clearly set out its jurisdiction over "the criminal law" and "procedure in criminal matters."

What would Lord Justice Sir Robert Megarry of the English Chancery Division make of all this? In 1983, he wrote:

> "As a matter of Law, the Courts of England recognize Parliament as being omnipotent in all save the power to destroy its own omnipotence."[4]

Meanwhile, here in Canada, our Parliament's omnipotence continues to have strips torn off it. In the *Tran* case, a rule of criminal procedure was virtually neutered – without so much as a peep of protest from our Honourable Members.

Our 1982 Charter of Rights envisaged a creative dialogue between elected representatives and the courts. The courts were specifically permitted to tell Parliament if it had constitutionally erred, and Parliament was encouraged to answer back. But this discourse has been all one way, with the courts making all the noise. Parliament has silently taken its lumps and then tried out new laws in an attempt to offset the social consequences of the courts' meddling.

The Charter, too, allows the people's representatives to prevail over decisions that perhaps make good legal sense but fly in the face of common sense. This is the purpose of Section 33, the "notwithstanding" clause – so Parliament can override Charter rights as interpreted by the Courts. This is similar to a retailer's guarantee – if people don't like what the judges sell them, they can return it and get their money refunded. Alas, our elected leaders have been too spooked and overawed by the Courts and the legal beagles to exercise their democratic recourse. It's high time they stopped being intimidated.

Non Judex in Causa Sua or a Possible Instance of Judging One's Own Case

Our poor Parliament – the people's forum – has already had its mustachios clipped by the Delilahs of Free Trade and NAFTA. Its authority over the criminal law has been slighted and spurned by judges, learned and zealous, but apt to overstep their bounds. Now we turn to yet another example of judicial interference.

Since Confederation, Parliament (and not the Cabinet) has set the salary scales and allowances of all Superior Court judges, usually after informal representation from bench and bar. This it has done under a clear mandate conferred by Section 100 of the 1867 Constitution. Likewise, provincial legislatures by law establish the pay and benefits of provincial court judges.

It is well accepted that very few wage-earners or salaried employees feel their pay measures up to what they deserve. Even some members of professional unions and professions cavil in this regard (medical doctors come to mind). Our contemporary justices, talented, honest and sincere and eager to seek the honour of judicial preferment, are human, and they, like others, may feel ill-served by their paymasters. But somehow, it seems, they are different, at least in their own minds. Their sole mistress should be the Law – "She who must be obeyed."

Of course inequities exist in the public sector, as they do to a greater extent in the private sector. Some civil service mandarins make more than Superior Court judges, and quite a number of others enjoy less arduous work and shallower responsibilities. A professional basketball player, on the carpet after a bar-room fracas, likely earns many times more than the judge who sentences him. But these disparities are essentially economic matters and must be redressed in the political arena. If the courts take on earnings determination, they will never get out of it.

The drafters of our Charter wisely left property rights and economic matters outside its purview, and that includes remuneration. Our Charter does not even provide for just compensation when property is expropriated: fairness is left to statute law. Neither can judges say who gets a taxi licence: that is left to the market, or to provincial commissions.

However, this state of affairs has led to unrest in some quarters, such as that of the Montreal provincial judges who deemed the loss of their parking privileges a Charter violation. Provincial governments across the country struggle to balance budgets by implementing cutbacks and freezes, a course of action which is seldom popular and often contentious – occasionally winding up in the courts. In the *Valente* case, the Supreme Court of Canada ruled that the government could downsize not only the court clerks but also others, including the judges. What governments could not do was discriminate against particular judges.

But *Valente* was to be reversed by the Court that decided it. In 1995 in Alberta, Premier Ralph Klein, citing red ink, decreed a general, temporary, five percent rollback in judges' pay. Some of his judges downed gavels, though they did not resign. The premier went on the air and said they must work or resign, and a constitutional challenge ensued.

The complainants found an ally in Justice McDonald of the Alberta Court of Queen's Bench. He took a long hard look at Section 100 of the Constitution, which says that Parliament shall "fix" the salaries and allowances of Superior Court judges. He formed the opinion that to "fix" salaries meant they could be raised but not lowered. If this was self-serving, it was also a blow to the long-held axiom that "no Parliament can bind its successor."

With Alberta in the final appeal were Manitoba and Prince Edward Island. The Supreme Court's judgement started off well, saying that "payments from the public purse are inherently a political issue." But it then lapsed into error, saying that Section 100 "guarantees the financial security of Supreme Court judges," which it does not. Then, the crux of the judgement relied on Section 11 (d) of the Charter, which states that "any person charged with an offence...has the right to be tried before an impartial tribunal." (It does not say to be tried before a happy judge.) But from this, the Court somehow inferred that Parliament and legislatures must refer changes in judicial salaries to an "independent body" to make non-binding recommendations. These changes must, however, be justified, if need be, in a court of law.[5]

The only dissenter was Justice LaForest, making the obvious point "that accused persons are the only beneficiaries of the rights set out in Charter Section 11 (d)."

But the damage was done. In telling elected members how they must go about deciding judicial salaries, and in saying that judges had the last word on what those salaries should be, the Court has strayed – for what any reasonable non-jurist would deem self-interest – a long, long way from any realistic reading of the Constitution.

Of Legal "Truth" and Consequences

In pre-Charter times, Parliament had rules for the determination of the status of refugees, those seeking admission to Canada because of a "well-founded fear of persecution" in their home countries. The procedure was sanctioned by the United Nations High Commission for Refugees and was similar to that commonly adopted in Western Europe. But in 1985, in *R v Singh* (1985, 1 SCR 177), the High Court struck down that procedure, giving all claimants the right to full oral hearings and court appeals, with benefit of counsel. The political fall-out was calamitous – not to mention the financial impact. In vain did Parliament attempt to contain the resultant constitutional mischief.

The *Singh* decision, which, almost two decades later, is still wreaking havoc, turned on three basic assumptions made by the majority judges:

- That the word "everyone" in the Charter's Fundamental Justice Section (Sec. 7) includes anyone who arrived at Canada's borders and claimed to be a refugee. As long as they touched Canadian soil and uttered the magic word "refugee," they were entitled to the Charter's protection – full legal rights and social equality.

- That saving time and money (described as avoiding "administrative inconvenience") could not be taken into account in deciding whether the procedures then in use were justifiable "in a free and democratic society."

- That those awaiting refugee hearings were constitutionally barred from deportation. Even if convicted of a crime in a Canadian court, the right to a hearing remained, funded by legal aid, as well as an appeal in the event of an adverse ruling to the Federal Court.

At the time of the *Singh* decision, 36,000 claimants were waiting to have their cases determined, and 7,000 unexecuted deportation orders were outstanding. The decision compounded the chaos. The numbers swelled as word of Canada's amazingly liberal position spread overseas. In vain did the government appoint 65 more refugee judges from among its party faithful. Immigration consultants charged needy supplicants fees of $1,000 and more. Unimpeachable stories were concocted, to be separated out, if at all possible, from stories of genuine fear of persecution. Genuine refugees lingered at the back of the queue, some stopped at sea or denied airplane boarding.

Singh had, ironically and possibly tragically, hobbled, not enabled, Parliament's ability to adopt fair investigative procedures. Sheer volume jammed immigration processes. In 1988, amnesties were granted to 15,000 applicants who were allowed to stay in Canada without further ado. Many would-be refugees were just buying time, up to five years, until their jig was up – at which point, they'd go to the press with their sad tales of being forced to leave a country where they'd by now perhaps borne children, some of whom were starting kindergarten.

As I write, one such wannabe Canuck, a member of a Hong Kong Triad underworld gang since his teens, is appealing, before a Canadian judge, the government's refusal to allow him entry. This gangster swears he has given up his Triad ways. But already, according to B.C.'s Co-ordinated Crime Unit, 800 Triad members have slipped into our country, busying themselves with loan-sharking, contract murders, home invasions, prostitution – all with an assist from *Singh*.

Recently, the Vancouver newspapers have been full of stories about young Honduran children, all recent arrivals on our shores, about half of them smuggled into the country, who are forced by their latter-day Fagans to sell crack cocaine on city streets using state-of-the-art team sales techniques. One solicits the customer and leads him to the dispenser. The dispenser sells a "rock" or two and turns over the cash to a cashier. Another holds inventory to replenish the dispenser's supply. A network of look-outs provides an early-warning system against police.

A model of industry this may be, but not one that ought to be encouraged. In the first nine months of 1998, 227 addicts, mostly young, died from cocaine overdoses in B.C. alone. Clogged courts and jails mean easy bail and short sentences for drug pushers.

In another case, a Vietnamese man arrived here in 1990, claiming to be a tourist. At the time of writing, he is in jail for 14 months pending his appeal of a deportation order. Previous to his jail term, he was collecting welfare while driving a flashy silver Toyota Camry. Police officers allege that he had been a gang leader in Vancouver. They say he was involved in a witness's "disappearance," had stabbed a restaurant owner, had torched another restaurant and had survived an attack on his own life and refused to identify the man who left him wounded. Eight years after setting foot on our shores, his deportation remains "under judicial review."[6]

Canada is scrambling for solutions, hamstrung by the *Singh* decision. Parliament, funked by a growing immigration "industry," has failed to use the Charter's "notwithstanding" clause to clear the decks and provide justice only to those with a genuine fear of persecution. How fair is all this to law-abiding Honduran and Vietnamese immigrants, and their communities, or to immigrants from anywhere, for that matter?

Inventing a Criminal Defence

Meanwhile, elsewhere, the High Court was again paying less than due respect to the will of Parliament. In 1990, it ruled that self-induced intoxication, by drink or drugs, could lead to acquittal in cases of sexual and other assaults. This new defence bears the imposing name of "non-insane automatism." It is judge-made law at its worst. Its appalling results were seen when a dangerous offender was cleared of a brutal rape after claiming he had had too much alcohol.

The drunkenness defence has quite a history. In 1989, a Supreme Court majority again affirmed that drunkenness was no excuse for such general-intent crimes as assault.[7] Intoxication remained, however, as a mitigating and important consideration in arriving at a proper sentence. This was consistent with the Common Law, which did not find guilty someone without guilty intent. In the words of the late, great Chief Justice of England, Edward Coke:

> "If one shoots at any wild fowl upon a tree, and the arrow killeth any reasonable creature afar off, without evil intent in him, this is *per infortunium.*"

That is, the poor chap has had terrible bad luck but can rightly be considered innocent.

But does this apply to someone who drinks himself into a mean, brutal mood and then rapes? This is not a case of *per infortunium;* the man who does this is not morally innocent. Convicting him of the assault may be rough justice, but it is commonsensical. Many crimes are committed by people out of their right minds, in a variety of degrees. The Law moves in the right direction when the important question becomes not one of morality, but of what to do with someone who has harmed another.

So the Court, in general, was affirming a clear parliamentary (and common-law) distinction between two kinds of criminal offences. In the first kind, including all bodily assaults, the guilty intent (or *mens rea*) was assumed from the carrying out of the assault itself. As the old common-law maxim has it, "A person is taken to intend the consequences of his own act."

The other kind of offence required the Crown to prove not only the actions of the offender but also a specific intent to commit the crime – for example, "assault with intent to resist arrest" or setting a fire "with intent to defraud" or having unprotected sex with another *knowing* that one was HIV-positive. Here, the Crown must show specific intent. Murder, of course, is a crime of specific intent.

The judges who upheld this distinction in 1989 considered that someone voluntarily zonking himself out and then attacking another was not morally innocent. He could not then claim a denial of fundamental justice. And further, as a practical matter, the real question was what the court should do with such offenders, who might very well go on to hurt someone else – or even themselves.

But some judges dissented. Convicting a person who did not appreciate what he was doing, they said, was a Charter violation. And, they added, "It is always open to the Court to overrule prior decisions where the effect is to establish a rule favourable to the accused."[8]

By 1990, with new appointments to fill vacancies, the dissenters commanded a majority on the Court. They proceeded to blur, if not obliterate, the Parliamentary distinction between crimes of *general* intent and crimes of *special* intent. They maintained that the Charter made them do this, although its broad words do no such thing but merely restate long-established law.

Mischief was afoot. Soon the Court found itself wrestling with the egregious proposition that drunkenness could be a defence to drunk driving.[9] For the time being, a very drunk accused driver did not get off. But it was a close call, with some judges saying that if the accused had been even drunker, he could have qualified as an *automaton*.

Then, in 1992, a Mr. Parks got away with murder. He said he had got out of bed, dressed himself, driven 23 kilometres across Toronto in the wee hours of the morning and stabbed his mother-in-law to death with a kitchen knife. He also stabbed his father-in-law, although the man survived. Parks claimed he did all this without waking up from a deep sleep. When he did finally come to, he dialed 911, telling the operator he had just killed two people "with his bare hands." A credulous jury, with the help of an expert in sleep disorders, acquitted Parks, and the Supreme Court upheld his sleep-walking defence, calling it "non-insane automatism."[10] Had Parks really murdered in his sleep? If so, it *would* be a defence, unlike intoxication.

So a new defence had been born and come of age. Experts were dredged up who were ready and willing to testify to the innocence of the accused. They could not, of course, be bought. But they could be rented – by those who could pay their healthy fees. They attested, in various venues, not only to sleep disorders but also to "cocaine psychosis" and "psycho-genetic and organic dissociative states." Drinking buddies now took the stand to sadly swear that their friend, the accused, had indeed had one too many. How long would it be before some clever fellow figured out he could put in a slurry-voiced call to 911, murder his girlfriend, knock off a bottle and get away free?

Not long. A 72-year-old man, Mr. Daviault, dropped in on a friend of his wife bearing a 40-ounce bottle of brandy. She was a partially paralyzed 65-year-old woman, confined to a wheelchair. She retired to her bedroom for the night, got up to go to the bathroom, was grabbed by Daviault, thrown on her bed and brutally raped. In the morning, a naked Daviault said he had finished the brandy before, not after, his heinous feat. Honest! The Supreme Court, in 1995, allowed his *automatism* defence, quashed his conviction, and granted him a re-trial.[11] Daviault's "pharmacological experts" chalked up a win.

Some judges dissented, maintaining that logic had run away with common sense. Justice Sopinka added, "It is not sound social policy to jettison a rule that has stood for 150 years." He was echoing Lord Russell, who said in *R v Morgan,* 1976 (House of Lords) A.C. 182, that "logic in criminal law must not be allowed to run away with common sense."

However, the Daviault case had pushed the envelope too far, tossing the justice minister, Alan Rock, on the waves of public indignation. The government had to act. The fair and simple way out was to re-pass the law of assaults, using the "notwithstanding" clause of the Charter.[12] But that would outrage vocal and influential criminal defence lawyers. Instead, Parliament resorted to a legal detour around the Daviault decision. It decreed that, henceforth, self-induced intoxication would not be a defence to assault, if the alcohol or other intoxicating substance taken departed "markedly" from "Canadian standards."[13]

But Parliament had scotched the automaton snake, not killed it – at least, not quite. It will not be beyond the genius of some lawyers to argue that their client had tripped out enough to be an "automaton" but had not "markedly" offended Canadian standards, whatever they may be. In some parts, Canadians drink (or shoot up) pretty heavily. If nothing else, such defences will kill precious court time in cases to come.

This Is No Who-Dunnit

Now for an open-and-shut murder case, one where the Supreme Court "read into" the Charter words that are not there, with calamitous effects upon the repute of the justice system.

But first, by way of introduction, some words from the Honourable Mr. Justice Hamish Gow, of the B.C. Supreme Court, of sensible Scots-Picts descent:

"Having a spurious reputation for omniscience, a few weeks ago I had a call from a lawyer, who, for the sake of his client, was anxious to suppress the truth and asked me if I knew of a helpful authority. I said, 'Of course. Look at *Feeney v The Queen,* 1997, 115 CCC (3rd), 129 (SCC).' Just the other day, he called me back to thank me, chortling over the success it had brought him. *Inter alia,* he said, "Its intellectual and verbal clamjamfray (see Chambers Dictionary) is scary, but, oh, what a tomb in which to bury the truth."[14]

Second, some words on the relevant law. Under Charter Section 9, a police officer cannot "arbitrarily" make an arrest. Nor, under Section 8, can an officer search a residence "unreasonably." This is simple enough law and easy to live with – far easier than what a judge in this case called "the recognized additions to the Charter words" – that is, promulgations by Courts without the blessing of elected representatives.

Our Charter, for one thing, says nothing about the need to obtain warrants. That is a matter regulated by ordinary statute law. (Not so in the U.S., where the Fourth Amendment states that "people are secure in their houses…and no warrant shall issue without probable cause…") Canada's omission makes good sense. An arrest or search can be "reasonable" without a warrant and "unreasonable" with one, and warrants may be unreasonably issued or unreasonably withheld. The fact remains that, without breaching the Charter, good evidence cannot be squelched.

Well, that is the theory, at least. In Michael Feeney's case, theory and practice parted company for good.

On June 8, 1991, in the isolated town of Likely (pop. 300) in B.C.'s Cariboo region, Feeney's day began well. In the morning, he played baseball. Later, he partied, did some drinking and that night, in a search for more beer, crashed his car in a ditch. He also broke into the home of 85-year-old Frank Boyle and, after killing his helpless victim with five blows of a crowbar, made off with $350 in cash and Boyle's car. He crashed Boyle's car in the same ditch and walked to his own trailer home, presumably to sleep it off.

Next morning, Boyle's friends alerted the police, who drove 75 miles from the detachment at Williams Lake to the scene. Several locals tipped them that Feeney was involved, and his car and his victim's appeared, from the skid marks, to have been ditched by the same person. Moreover, he had been seen walking home to his trailer from Boyle's abandoned car.

The officers received no answer when they knocked on the door of Feeney's windowless trailer and shouted "Police!" Entering, they found Feeney sound asleep in a blood-spattered room and woke him up. After giving him the caution, they asked how he came to have blood all over himself and were told he'd been hit while playing baseball. Questioned further, Feeney said he had struck Boyle and directed the officers to the stolen money under his mattress. He was arrested and the evidence seized. The blood was later matched to that on Boyle's refrigerator.

At the RCMP detachment, Feeney made more admissions. At trial, he was convicted of second-degree murder, reduced from first-degree because of his drinking. The B.C. Court of Appeal affirmed the conviction.

Then the Supreme Court got its hand on the case. Unbelievably, it found the officers had violated no less than four sections of the Charter. The Court – by a slim five-to-four majority – suppressed all the evidence found, bloody shirt and all, and excluded all Feeney had said at the time of his arrest.

The Charter infractions cited by a majority of the Court raised the bars that police and prosecutors must jump. These infractions included the following.

- The officers had not stated the purpose of their knock, nor waited long enough for a response.

- The caution did not say enough about telephoning a lawyer (although there was no phone, and Feeney, when asked if he understood the caution, had replied, "I am not illiterate").

- The arresting sergeant had no "subjective" belief that he had cause to enter and collar Feeney. At one point during cross-examination, this officer said he thought he had; at another point that he thought he had not. (He either knew too much or too little about criminal cases.)

- The sergeant also failed to pass the "objective" test, with the Court finding he and his colleagues had acted only on suspicion, together with their belief that they had to act before evidence was destroyed and had to quickly determine if the killer was in the trailer or on the loose.

- The sergeant had not acted in "good faith"; he had not followed the Law as the Court was, with embellishments, laying it down.

- The officers had not, in what they thought was an emergency, stopped to apply for a warrant – a warrant for which there was no provision in the Criminal Code – and this was not a case of "hot pursuit."

- Given that the arrest was unlawful, the police at the detachment had no right to take Feeney's fingerprints.

As if all this were not enough, the Court also stated that the detachment officers had no right to breathalyze Feeney, although the fact that he was over the limit helped reduce his initial sentence.

Calling these violations "very, very serious," the Court suppressed every whit of crucial evidence, apparently to preserve the Law's repute. The whole shooting match, they declared, was "derivative" of Charter breaches.

Not surprisingly, the four dissenters entered a vigorous, passionate response. Speaking for them, Madam Justice L'Heureux-Dubé wrote that the majority seemed to think the officers "were acting as lawless vigilantes," adding that it was "impractical to get a warrant in that isolated community." She noted that locating and neutralizing the killer, as well as gathering evidence, had been a matter of some urgency, and that the officers, "for their foresight, should be commended, not rebuked."

To this I would add that the majority reasons had nothing to do with preventing innocent people from wrongful conviction, which is the standard rationale of those who uphold Court additions to the Constitution.

The Court ordered a re-trial. But with the Crown shorn of so much of its evidence and the arresting officers forced to feign blindness and deafness (in effect lying to the judge), it was a bit of a sham. Nonetheless, in February 1999, after six and a half days of deliberation, the B.C. Supreme Court jury found Feeney guilty, nearly *seven years* after his original conviction.

Does the risk of letting a brutal killer free over a legal nicety matter? Of course it does. It lowers respect for the courts, and citizens have every right to complain about the costs entailed. Bad publicity hurts. Dangerous precedents are set and uncertainties proliferate.

Meanwhile, the government has responded to public outrage by passing make-do laws, seeking to restore the previous common-law powers of arrest and seizure. Forced to tread carefully, they are making the Law needlessly complex. Unable actually to reverse the court findings of constitutional violation, they hope that their efforts will withstand further court scrutiny. They appear to be unwilling, however, to resort to the "notwithstanding" section of the Constitution, which was custom-made for this ruling.

On a happier note, I quote from the speech that our friend Justice L'Heureux-Dubé, that sensible woman, gave to the 26th Canadian Congress of Criminal Justice in Ottawa in 1997. Emphasizing that the search for truth is the very purpose of criminal justice, she quoted Justice Byron White of the U.S. Supreme Court, as follows:

"Civilized society must maintain its capability to discover transgressions of the Law and identify those who flout it."

She added that, "while the Charter rights of the accused are part of the equation, they are not all of the equation." Let's face it – far, far too much has been "read in" to our criminal law, far beyond the Charter's words and Parliament's will.

Diminished Responsibility

Canadian criminal justice has been too preoccupied lately with the trial process. Sentencing is the Law's greatest challenge – creating dispositions that fit the circumstances of the offender as well as the offence, while keeping public safety firmly in mind.

Many of those charged with serious personal-injury offences, as well as with such minor offences such as threatening and petty theft, have some degree of psychiatric disorder or mental infirmity. Jailing them protects the public only until their sentences are over. And jails have a way of releasing more proficient and more violent criminals. Funds to build more jails would be better spent on alternatives to custody for those who pose little risk to the public, and for compulsory hospital confinement and treatment for some of those who do pose serious risks.

Fortunately, Parliament is moving in this direction. Since 1992, law-breakers can be found to be "not criminally responsible on account of mental disorder." [15] "Automatons" would not come under this section unless their defence arose from mental disease. When so found, a defendant can receive an absolute discharge if – in the discretion of the judge – he or she is unlikely to re-offend. Or the defendant can be committed for assessment, hospital confinement and treatment. This approach contrasts with the populist demand for mandatory minimum sentences, which takes no account of the personality of the accused or the risk he or she poses to others.

But this new sentence option must go back into parliamentary committee for repairs. The vague words, "mental disorder," can be stretched to include every kind of personality defect. The prestigious American Psychiatric Association even lists anti-social psychopaths among those who can be found "not criminally responsible." Society cannot afford to give that protection to persons whose callous lack of concern for others is expressed in violence. These folks have to realize there are penal consequences, no matter how muddled their minds.

Moreover, procedural safeguards must be added. A knockabout adversarial contest, with each side purchasing expert witnesses, is not the best way to make a correct diagnosis of a medical condition. Not surprisingly, with the section as it stands, defence lawyers are increasingly able to play games with jurors' heads.

Not that all jurors can't get it right, as the Dorothy Joudrie affair illustrates. In 1994 Mrs. Joudrie, a Calgary socialite, shot her estranged husband six times as he lay on the floor of her home. Her actions bore all the outward marks of cold-blooded premeditation. But she had been sorely beset by severe, prolonged depression and delusions. The jury, finding "mental disorder," was right to assign her to custodial treatment followed by supervised release. Had Joudrie been able to invoke successfully the "non-insane automatism" defence, she would have simply been acquitted, with no follow-up treatment.

In Great Britain today, many "guilty" offenders with emotional and psychological infirmities are referred to judges out of the criminal justice system, under the Mental Health Act. This Act authorizes sufficient custody and treatment to secure, as best as mortals can acting humanely, the safety of the public.

But back in Canada, consider the troublesome case of Wayne Sullivan, to choose one example from too many. Sullivan was a pulp mill mechanic in

Prince George, B.C. In 1992, he and his wife were in a pub when they were joined by the wife's girlfriend. Drinking and dancing took place, with Sullivan downing plenty of beer. The three then drove to the Sullivan home, where Wayne proposed a sexual threesome. Rebuffed in this erotic proposal, he followed his wife into the bedroom, where (and we have only his word for this) she told him, "I don't love you. It's my girlfriend I love. Now go to bed."

Instead, he went to the basement, returned with a gun and shot his wife dead with a bullet to her head. Next, he raped the girlfriend at gunpoint, and then dialled 911. Arrested, he admitted responsibility for shooting his wife, adding, "I just fucked up." Later, however, he was to say he hadn't remembered a thing until months later, when a tire iron fell on his foot at work.

At trial, Sullivan mounted what was close to the best defence money could buy. His lawyer called a forensic psychiatrist who deposed that Mrs. Sullivan's profession of love for her girlfriend had catapulted her husband into "psychological automatism." A clinical psychologist testified that Sullivan had been "dissociated." Both said that the defendant had been forthright and had not exaggerated the story on which they based their opinions.

The prosecution was out-gunned, as well as taken by surprise. It scrambled and came up with a psychologist who didn't help much by explaining Sullivan's behaviour as an "alcoholic amnesiac episode."

Sullivan, found not 'criminally responsible', is now on probation, reporting periodically to a psychiatrist. The girlfriend, disbelieving and embarrassed, decided to leave town.[16]

Some citizens can be forgiven for doubting that a man who had just proposed sex à trois suddenly lost it when his wife declared a fondness for lesbian love.

The Sullivan case highlights some serious procedural issues. For one, the prosecution was clearly sandbagged. These lawyers should have received copies of the expert opinions well before trial. One-sided disclosure impairs truth-finding. (Given more time for research, they may have pointed out, for example, that the American Psychiatric Association states that the rare state of dissociation does not occur when the subject is intoxicated.)

Second, the defence was able to pay top dollar to its experts, while the prosecution was limited to a tariff of $150 an hour. All expert witnesses should be paid comparable fees, preferably funded by Legal Aid or some other public source.

Third, the defence was able to select and call only those experts who could be counted on to support the "disassociation" theory. Experts should all be chosen by the judge from a panel of certified and disinterested professionals. At the least, there should be early and full disclosure of expert reports obtained by either side.

Equality between prosecution and defence in the presentation of fact and opinions is more likely to result in truth. Sullivan's case involved the determination of a state of mind and the diagnosis of a psychiatric condition. That should have taken the form of an inquiry, with the judge having the right to call for more information at his or her discretion.

Nevertheless, by moving toward the concept of "diminished responsibility," Parliament had taken a significant step in the right direction. As for the courts, they should not spin superfluous complexities in criminal law, while paying too little attention to the best of public opinion as it is reflected in laws passed in the Parliament that Canadians elect.

Chapter 5

Under No Obligation

"[I] content myself with wishing that I may be one of those
whose follies may cease with their youth, and not of that
number who are ignorant in spite of their experience."

– William Pitt, 1741

Suppose, Dear Reader, you are made a youth-court judge for a day. You are trying a young woman – a very young woman, just 14 – for impaired driving. (Politically correct to a fault, you resist calling her a girl.) A police officer swears on the Bible and deposes as follows:

"I was on patrol on the evening of June 14, 1992, in Saskatoon, when I saw this young driver and suspected she had no licence. I pulled her over, and no, she hadn't. Plus her breath reeks of alcohol. I take her in the cruiser to the 7-Eleven, where she says her mom works, but I can't persuade the mother to leave her job and come with us to the station. However, she agrees to try to phone the accused's brother to go instead.

At the station, the youngster 'declines to exercise her right to counsel.' She takes the breath test and is over the limit. At that point her brother, I hear, has come into the waiting room. We proceed with a second, cautionary breath test…"

Defence counsel is immediately on his feet with an objection. "Brother not let in for second test! Test must be excluded and charge dismissed! I can quote precedents!" He does so. (*Therens* lives.)

You, the judge, listen, with one ear, your mind adrift. When will we get to what really matters? So young, drinking and driving. What's at the root of this? Family troubles? Bad company? Not making it at school? Some pang or other that youth are heir to? You want to hear all you can. Instead, the defence lawyer is saying his client will not be taking the stand, "on advice of counsel." Then – strange, this – he quotes a case with exactly the same facts as the one you are hearing (*R v I [P.R.], SQB 1992, 78 CCL* [3rd] 442). Like a good judge, you follow precedents, rejecting the second test and acquitting the accused.

But you can't shake the uneasy feeling that the law has let you down. You give the youngster a warning – though not a lecture, not to an "innocent" person – and feel a bit better. But you wonder what the youngster feels – more respect for justice, or less?

I was but 11 years old when I had my first (and last) confrontation with the criminal justice system. My memory kindly blurs the details of my crime. I think I had climbed a grouchy neighbour's tree and stolen apples. But I vividly recall my correction. My father, a judge, quietly arranged for a constable to pay me a visit. This fellow loomed above me, bluff, corpulent and burly, a cop right out of Central Casting. After subjecting me to a stern interrogation, he left me with dire visions of lock-ups.

Now surely this process was simpler and more to the point than the young woman's drunk-driving case. It nipped my criminal career in the bud. Probably, although I'm guessing, the constable, once out of sight, enjoyed a chuckle.

Toward Youth Justice Tailored to the Criminal Model

In 1984, Canada's parliamentarians, perhaps inebriated by their exuberance for rights, replaced the Juvenile Delinquents Act of 1908 with the Young Offenders Act. It was as if they'd heard the word from on high: "Come to the Charter waters! Drink and your souls shall live!"

The new legislation reflects a new philosophy, as well as, in procedure, a change that is still picking up pace. The old JD Act was primarily concerned with the individuality of the young delinquent and his or her reformation.

The new act focuses more on the crime, and on a punishment to fit the crime. In addition, the youth court has seen a new group of players. There are more lawyers, and fewer counsellors, social workers, probation officers or other professionals knowledgeable in mental and emotional disorders.

Father Time, too, plays a much bigger role. Trials grow longer and the gap between offence and trial widens, to the point where the average is now one year. This is long enough for the young culprit to lose any contrition, or empathy for his victims, that he may have felt at his arrest. And it's long enough for him to think that his trial, though based on past misdeeds, was more of an event reconstructed with legal assistance. The court climate has altered, as well, as informality gives way to its opposite.

Costs, too, have risen – something many citizens would not mind so much if youth social programs to prevent crime were equally well – or even adequately – funded, which they are not. And strangely, the number of young offenders held in detention centres, both before and after trial, has soared. These centres allow youngsters to mingle with other mischief-makers, as well as some who are truly dangerous to themselves, the public and their fellow inmates. Why this jump in numbers? Perhaps the times are out of joint, or the new system is somehow responsible. In any case, we'd be wise to divert far more young people safely out of the system, instead of letting them get caught up in it – worse for the experience.

The centrepiece of the Young Offenders Act is its Section 556, as it was renumbered in 1998. A subsection reads:

> "The young person is under no obligation to give a statement to a police officer."

Now, what kind of signal is this to send to teens? It expresses one of the shibboleths of our Law, one which the criminal defence bar is apparently prepared to defend to the death. Never mind that it contradicts the wisdom of the ages when it comes to raising youngsters into responsible adulthood.

So, as we are seeing, the law offers young offenders two ways to escape responsibility for their mistakes. The first, passed by Parliament, allows them to refuse to answer a police officer's questions about wrong-doing in which they may have been involved. The second, judge-made, places no onus on them to explain to a court what they've been up to – even after a fair, though not conclusive, case has been presented against them.

Allowing youthful miscreants to refuse to answer questions posed by the police, as permitted by Canada's notorious Young Offenders Act, sends a dangerous message to teenagers in trouble with the law. Most lawyers, alas, believe that the right to silence is in the best interest of both society and young people. No sensible parent could agree with them.

Suppose you are a mom or dad of a young person under age 18. You start to feel your teenager may be mixed up in some trouble – perhaps in petty theft from school lockers, perhaps cheating on exams, perhaps a fracas in a mall. You decide to have a heart-to-heart with the kid. "Tell me all about it," you say. "Come clean." After all, your child's future may be on the line, and you may have to dole out some discipline.

Sensible parents know that the first step in correcting youthful misbehaviour is getting the miscreant to own up. And they know that acknowledging wrong-doing is in the best interests of the young person, since it minimizes the chance that the offender will repeat.

Sadly, the federal government's lawmakers have yet to grasp this concept. The whole wide world knows that confessing is good for the soul. So why doesn't the Law get it? Surely a duty to speak up serves young people in trouble better than a right to keep mum.

Diminishing the Role of Conscience

This "no obligation" rule plays out in many ways. Take the case of young "Peter Williams" (the young miscreant's name has been changed to protect the guilty). His was no petty offence. He was party to a vicious murder and robbery. After his arrest, some moral urge prompted Peter to confess and expiate, at least to some extent, a terrible deed. He wanted to talk, to try to put the matter behind him and clear his conscience. The Law thought it knew better.

Peter's case began in 1988 and dragged on for five years, when the Supreme Court finally entered an acquittal.[1]

The story is this. In the wee hours of October 12, 1988, this young man (then 16 and a school drop-out) and two of his friends, aged 17 and 23, took a cab from the native reserve at Duncan, B.C., to Victoria, some 65 kilometres to the south. They had been partying hard and had several drinks en route to their destination. In their possession were two mean-looking pellet guns, two "throwing knives" and what the 23 year old later called "tools to break and enter."

Arriving in Victoria about 4 a.m., the threesome asked to stop at a boot-legger's for two cases of beer. After paying off the cabby, they hung out downtown, talking about how to get some money. Since, at that hour, taxi drivers were almost the only people around, they decided to rob one. Hailing another cab, they jumped in and set off for a remote area. The two in the back seat stuck their guns in the driver's neck, but the driver resisted. In the scuffle for the driver's wallet, Peter, who was in the front seat, stabbed him several times. The man died.

At a friend's house, the young men washed the blood from their cloth-ing, but some remained on Peter's. Later that day, one of the youths casually mentioned that they'd killed a cabby. The RCMP were tipped, and all three were arrested.

At the lock-up, Peter was given the Charter caution and was told to call a lawyer and have a guardian come down. (He chose a great-aunt.) However, before the lawyer arrived (the great-aunt was there), one Constable Logan engaged Peter in a long conversation. Before it was over, Peter told Logan something of what had happened. The other two youths were to hold guns to the cabby's neck. Peter was supposed to sit in the front seat and "just stab." Logan then drove Peter to a house where he produced the fatal knife and the cabby's car keys. Later that day, at Logan's urging, he talked with his lawyer.

The next morning, Peter had another phone conversation with his lawyer. Then, seeing Logan, he told the officer that he had left out some details and wanted to add more. Again the two men spoke, and again Peter confessed, possibly embellishing his story, for now he said the plan was to rob and kill.

On legal advice, Peter did not testify at his trial in youth court. He was found guilty of second-degree murder, and the verdict was affirmed by the appeal court. However, in 1993, the Supreme Court set aside the judgement.

Now, to my mind, the courts had before them a grave human and social problem. They treated this problem, however, strictly as a question of law – as if what really mattered was what label to pin on Peter: "guilty" or "not guilty"?

In legal terms, the Supreme Court had these conundrums to solve. The first, concerning Peter's admissions to the police before his lawyer arrived, was easily decided. His admissions were irregular. But wait – would he have made the later admission if he had not made the earlier one? The court said no, so that both were out of order.

The Court had no doubt that Peter's statements were basically true, and that Logan had been frank and polite in all his dealings with the youth. Nevertheless, it held that Logan had slipped up in the way he'd obtained the admissions. Therefore, the words had to be treated as if they'd never been spoken. To do otherwise would sully the Law's fair name. Not surprisingly, the Court did not quote the dictum of the eminent American jurist, Justice Benjamin Cardozo, who said: "The criminal must go free, because the constable has blundered."[2]

Of course, Cardozo had used these words ironically, adding: "One sin does not cancel out another." But our Court followed his dictum as if it made good sense. They freed Peter because of Logan's blunder.

Let me say, since this needs stressing, that police blunders, misconduct and abuses always pose a threat to a free society. But they should be checked directly, by wise, thorough civilian overseers, along with constant upgrading in the selection and training of peace officers, continuing education and a judicious, no-nonsense Ombudsperson who is outside the system and empowered to hear and redress grievances, reporting to Parliament and the provincial legislatures. But we should not try to police the police by court rejection of reliable evidence. Some courts throw out evidence to "teach the police a lesson," others to "deny police the 'fruits' of their misconduct." Others simply want to improve the Law's image, so they say. This practice not only disheartens police officers, who have trouble enough trying to cope with the mad, the bad and the sad in the community, but it is also likely to lead to surreptitious abuses.

Nor can it be proved that rejecting evidence curbs police abuses. In the U.S., where suppression of evidence is viewed as an integral part of legal sparring, research shows that it has not led to any significant decrease in illegal police practices.[3]

But to return to Peter's case: the upshot was clearly that three young men had committed murder - at least second-degree murder. Their individual complicity might have varied some, but that ought to have been a matter for sentencing.

Clearing Peter meant that the Court did not have to deliberate on the really serious issue in his case. It was Peter who had been on trial, not Peter's crime. So questions about his background, motives and personality were ignored. Who was he? Why had he taken part in this crime? Did he feel remorse? Would he, after serving prison time, be likely to re-offend?

In youth court, matters are not quite as cut and dried as they may be when adults are being tried. As Julian Mack, an American scholar, puts it, "The problem for determination by the Judge is not only, has this boy or girl committed a specific wrong, but what is he, how has he become what he is, and what had best be done, in his interest and in the interest of the State, to save him from a downward career."[4]

These questions, social and human as they are, do belong in courtrooms. And the answers to them will only be found in a quest for as much of the whole truth as it is possible to come by. Criminal cases, especially those concerning young people, must slide away from the adversarial model, with its gladiatorial combats and prosecutors devising strategies to out-manoeuvre those of the defence. The presiding judge should lead an inquiry, independently if need be, of the two sides – more inquisitorial and less adversarial.

"Legal fairness," as in Peter's case, all too often gets the better of truth-seeking. And ignoring truth can grease the slippery slope on which a young lawbreaker finds himself, hastening a life-destroying future as a criminal.

To a Downward Career?

A young man in Lethbridge, Alberta, was thought to be trading in drugs. Was it really better for all concerned to sweep the truth under the rug? Narcotics officers, with a warrant, searched his home. They found no physical evidence. However, during the search, the suspect gave himself away with something he said. He was escorted to the station house and given the usual cautions – "No obligation…right to a lawyer and guardian…" and so on. Then he was asked to sign the Young Offenders Act "waiver," which he did, but not without adding the words: "I do not wish to say anything further until I talk to a lawyer."

To this, an officer responded by telling him to go home, adding, "I will have to talk to your brother Gary to see if further charges should be laid." This led the young man into more admissions.

When the case reached the Alberta appeal court, however, it ruled that the constable's words "had the effect of continuing a conversation that should have terminated." That blunder acquitted the young accused.[5] Did he leave the courtroom chastened? Or thinking, "I got away with it, must be more careful next time"?

"Saved" by the Charter

As if the Young Offenders Act were not causing enough trouble in the courts, its tenets have been adopted in some schools. A 13-year-old Alberta lad, with an assist from some classmates, stole money from his teacher's purse when she left the room to attend a brief meeting. On her return, she found the open purse on her desk and reported the theft to the principal. She then told her class that if the culprits owned up and returned the money, nothing more would be done about it. They came forward. But the principal, knowing nothing of this promise, called the youngsters into his office, elicited further confessions and called the Law.

Arraigned in Youth Court, our 13-year-old was let off.[6] The Judge ruled that his Charter rights had been abridged; that both the teacher and principal had been "persons in authority"; that the boy had been "detained"; and that he had not been cautioned that he could "say nothing, but that if he did, it could be used against him." Nor was he advised of his right to counsel. Therefore, to find him guilty would bring justice into disrepute.

Of course, the teacher's promise *had* been broken, and she would have some explaining to do to her class. But the pupils also had a duty – to own up, promise or no promise. That should have been part of the teacher's explanation. As to the principal, he had no business calling in the police, unless this youngster was a persistent young thief, which he was not. The principal should have put the fear of God into him, ordered some after-class detention time and reported the whole sorry tale to his parents. A court visit, especially one that ended in acquittal, was no way to teach him respect for others. His own "I'm sorry" would have been a better education.

By 1997, thankfully, an Ontario judge did decide that a principal's authority extended to searches of students suspected of bringing drugs to school. But then, giving his good sense some time off, the judge added, "but not if [the principal] enlists the aid of a police officer." The good judge was pronouncing on a case in which a crimestopper tip had alerted police to a student who put drugs in a pocket of his red jacket to smuggle into his high school. An officer visited the principal, and together they checked the student's locker. No red jacket. The pair proceeded to the gym, where they saw the jacket hanging, and spoke to the student, who – knowing the game was up – said, "You'll find it in my jacket." They did.

However, the mere presence of a policeman stuck in the judge's craw. Moreover, no cautions had been made, no suggestion to the student of his right to counsel, etc., etc. Evidence of both words and drugs was suppressed and the student acquitted.[7]

Odd, is it not, that a high-school principal can proceed on "mere suspicion," but a police officer cannot? We pay officers to enforce the law, and then hobble them more than someone we pay to administer a place of learning. As for drugs, not to mention knives, in our schools, this is scary stuff – and becoming pretty common, according to my young grandsons. Can guns be far behind? A headline in a British newspaper, *The Independent* (May 23, 1998), states that in the United States in 1997, 6,000 students were expelled for taking guns to school.

But onward, to a new cast of characters: two caring parents; their son, "George," aged 14; the accused, "John," a young 15-year-old stray who had left his home and was kindly allowed by George's mom and dad to stay in their home; and a judge who knew more than enough Charter law.

In 1996, George and John donned masks and, armed with knives, robbed a convenience store in Etobicoke, Ontario. Fleeing, George dropped his wallet near the store. This brought officers to call on mom and dad. Mom made sure George had a chat with the officers, who produced his wallet. He admitted to the robbery and implicated John as well.

John was questioned. Knowing George has ratted on him, John told the officers that "it wasn't a balaclava – we wore stockings." Months later, he was videotaped by police, telling all. He also agreed to testify against George in a plea bargain and was subsequently let go with 18 months' probation.

In 1997, George went to trial with two strikes against him. But the judge excluded his confession, saying George had felt intimidated by the officers. Next, the judge rejected John's evidence against George, which he held to be "derivative of George's conscripted admission." That is, John would not have tattled on his pal if George hadn't first got them both into trouble. George went free.

Now back to mom, who had ensured her son cooperated with the officers. Did she think that it would have been better for her son to face the music, pay his social debt and get on with his life? Or would she agree that the Charter knew better?

The Winnipeg Connection

Here we have a nasty crime and a severely dysfunctional, high-risk young offender. Surely, releasing him into the community would be unthinkable. Yet, though the truth was never in doubt, the courts spent the next seven years navigating through Charter shoals, barely missing the rocks.

In 1984, "Joe," a 17-year-old Winnipeg lad, brutally raped and murdered a three-year-old girl. Her body was found in a garage, blue panties at her feet, her rectum torn and bruised, her skill fractured and her neck broken.

As soon as the body was found, the police began to round up possible witnesses, among them this 17 year old. Attending at the police station, Joe gave an account of his whereabouts that, checked out, proved to be false. He also tried to shift the blame onto someone else.

The young man was confronted with shreds of scalp and clothing that could be his. Again, he tried to pin the crime on another, saying, "Yeah, like I said, he took her to a garage and she was crying for her grandmother" – details that could only have been known by the guilty person. He then conceded, "I grabbed her...took her to the garage...blacked out."

The police ceased their questioning, arrested Joe and read him his Charter rights. He conferred with his lawyer for 37 minutes. When she left, not asking the officers to stop any further questioning, the police resumed their inquiries. Once more, Joe voluntarily admitted to the crime. On the way to the detention centre, he pointed out the apartment building where he abducted her, pointed to the garage where he bludgeoned her to "stop her screaming" and even pointed out the bloody cinder block he used.

At the trial, which was held in adult court, the judge let the jury hear Joe's tape-recorded admissions, which he'd made prior to his lawyer's visit. But what he said and what he pointed out to the police *after* seeing his lawyer were ruled out. Joe was convicted of first-degree murder.

The matter went to appeal, where the court ruled just the opposite, rejecting Joe's admissions made before seeing his lawyer and allowing everything he said and did afterwards. A new trial was ordered, where – needless to say – he was once more convicted.

But this second trial was also appealed, and the court contradicted its earlier decision. This time, it excluded everything Joe *said* but admitted the gestures he made when he pointed out the apartment and garage to the police. Yet another trial was ordered, on manslaughter only.

But in 1991 – seven years after the crime had been committed – the case was sent to the Supreme Court, which ruled out *all* Joe said or did, both words and gestures. Again, a third trial was ordered, on manslaughter only, because there was still some evidence on which a jury could convict. What this was can only be guessed at – perhaps the shreds of scalp and clothing.[8]

The appeal court judges were unanimous, with the exception of Madam Justice L'Heureux-Dubé, that fount of common sense. She voted to sustain a conviction, vigorously deploring the way Truth and Law had drifted apart over seven years, like two ships caught in strong tidal currents, and calling attention to the stress passing time had inflicted on the bereaved family.

More Law, less Justice. What on earth could be "fair" about the third trial? What Winnipeg juror would not know, or not be told, that the accused had long ago confessed. And wouldn't you know it – Joe was convicted again.

One of the few violent and truly dangerous young offenders in the annals of Canadian law, Joe should be incarcerated until no longer a measurable risk to society – and if ever released, be subject to strict and vigilant probation. That much is clearly self-evident. But how many reasonable citizens would ever have imagined it would have taken the courts more than seven years to come to this conclusion?

Sense in Sentencing

I can't resist reflecting on this topic, although my brief really concerns court process. Canada has the third highest rate of youth incarceration in the Western world.[9] But crowded teen jails, with their bullies and gang members, do not improve conduct. Instead, these institutions serve as finishing schools, where hardened young thugs offer instruction in criminal techniques and ridicule those who seek self-improvement. Peer abuse includes thefts, calling-down, quick punches and sexual assault. Guards can't be everywhere, and there are no safe retreats.

This is clearly shown by the notorious case of John Dillinger. While still a teenager, he held up a storekeeper in Indiana. After 10 years of hard time in the penitentiary, Dillinger graduated in the 1930s to become a multiple killer, famous as America's "Public Enemy No. 1." He was finally gunned down by G-men.

We can usually identify the origins of anti-social behaviour: neglect or abuse at home; family breakdown; financial stress; learning disabilities; mental disorders. As W. H. Auden wrote in his poem, *September, 1939,* "Those to whom evil is done/Do evil in return." Most young offenders have also never had reasonable access to paid work.

In practice, criminal courts try persons, not crimes. Does it not seem essential to find out a little about the defendants' histories? Are they all callous hit-men and vicious sociopaths? A few are, and they must be held in close custody until they are no longer dangerous, usually in their senior years.

Would giving Peter (the Native youth), for example, a long stretch in one of our present overcrowded teen jails improve his conduct? Better a wilderness camp, like Boulder Creek in B.C.'s Fraser Valley, a remote spot in the trackless forest with one long, easily patrolled, dirt road out. At such camps, youngsters are up at 5 a.m. for a dip in the lake before a daily regimen of work, training and education. In a perfect world, this stint would be followed by probation and/or community service under a probation officer without too big a caseload - one who doesn't tolerate foolishness. As a bonus to the taxpayer, probation costs about a third less than warehousing a prison inmate.

Some naive souls see safety in longer sentences. Let them look south of the border, where California has more people locked up than all of Western Europe, Japan, Australia, New Zealand and Canada combined. Ironically, California is the least safe state of them all.

In Peter's case, the system clearly failed. The entire process was undermined by a dangerous notion: that citizen rights can be meaningful without citizen responsibilities, and that people have "no obligation" to answer to law-enforcement officers if doing so could land them in trouble.

As if the justice system came for free! No system does. There are costs to be paid in return for social justice and safe neighbourhoods – costs that must be shouldered by all, including witnesses and suspects.

Of course, there is only so much the justice system can do about the present disturbing rise in juvenile violence. A lot of it comes from thrown-away kids, and much of it is against each other. (There is nothing like senseless violence to snap you out of a depression.) Some seek to "belong" among their dysfunctional peers through bad behaviour, and some have reached their teens believing there is absolutely nothing wrong with theft, assault and other petty criminal activities. For too many young people, car theft, either for joy-riding or for sale to older sponsors, is a fashionable rite of passage.

The current rhetoric from the law-and-order populists denigrates what they view as bleeding-heart liberals' concerns about perpetrators' well-being. "What about the victim?" is the new rallying cry. Of course, victims must be heard from, kept informed and encouraged to speak up in the criminal justice process. But, especially in the case of young offenders, we must not let it become unfashionable to talk about the lousy home life or shoddy parenting suffered by many.

Preventing crime isn't as simple as the lock-'em-up crowd appears to believe. Deterrence springs from swift criminal process and short, humane, though sharp, penalties. A long game of legalistic point-scoring played between Crime and Punishment does nothing to deter criminal behaviour.

There is no alternative to preventive jailing for young persons who repeat vicious violence or commit sexual assaults. But whenever possible, they should serve their time in wilderness camps or something similar.

But alternatives to our trial system should be sought for young offenders. A young First Nations lad, for instance, could have been diverted from the usual criminal process. He had broken into the pool room on his reserve in Manitoba and stolen $65. His only violence was to the lock, which he smashed. He was tried and acquitted, on appeal, in the courts – a police constable's "blunder" did the trick, with the truth never an issue.[10]

It would have been better for all concerned if the prosecutor or judge had referred the youth's case to a hearing by his band's elders or to a "healing circle" – a group of band members who would meet with him and decide appropriate restitution or compensation he ought to make to expiate his crime. There, face to face with some of those he had hurt, he'd have a better appreciation of their concerns. He'd likely have to perform some community service by way of reconciliation. But he'd feel less of a "bad person" than he would have going through the courts, even though he got off. And he'd be far less likely to re-offend. Think of the cost savings – not to mention the increased chance to build the youth's character and sense of respect for others.

Of course, those elders would have insisted that all the truth came out. They'd have expected him to speak up and would have agreed completely with the principle expressed by the eminent Madam Justice Mary Southin of the B.C. Court of Appeal.:

> "A wise parent who suspects his child is up to no good does his best to ferret out the truth. He does not advise the child that he has a right to remain silent."[11]

Unfortunately, there's not much the Courts can do about contemporary social attitudes, which are marked by an increasing concern for self and much less for the well-being of others. But they and the lawmakers can do something, and should.

The "no obligation" section should be amended along these lines: "Young persons, and others, have an obligation when called upon courteously and without duress by a peace officer to say what they may know about criminal activity, whether as witnesses or as participants. Failure to speak candidly could count against them if they are brought to trial."

There is something odd about the judge-made reverse-onus doctrine. In one breath, a judge says, "Ah, some obligation on the accused! That violates the Constitution!" And in the next breath, he may say, "Still, it makes so much sense that it does not violate the Constitution!" It's a paradox, and one that leaves a lot of discretion to judges to pass over Parliament's wishes, adding uncertainties to the law and providing more grist to keep the mills of justice turning.

No Onus to Explain

The "no obligation" rule is a poor cousin to another tenet of our justice system, the "no reverse onus" rule. Not long ago, it was acceptable under certain sections of the Criminal Code for the accused to be called upon to offer a reasonable explanation of the evidence presented by the Crown. Today, however, many judges frown on putting any burden on the accused to respond with some defence or excuse. But whittling away such so-called reverse onus from criminal cases has grave social consequences.

Take the case of George Raymond, a devotee of the all-too-common activity of home burglary. Raymond was no longer a young offender when he was tried one sunny day in May 1994, in Vancouver Provincial Court.

During his trial, a police officer made oath and told how he and his partner had been parked in their patrol car, lights out, in a residential area, when they observed a blue Pontiac moving slowly down the block. The driver was glancing around as if searching for an address. But the officer, drawing on his experience, suspected the person behind the Pontiac's wheel might be looking for an unoccupied house.

After pulling the car over on the pretense of a malfunctioning tail-light, the officer made a routine check on the driver. He also noticed a steel bar projecting from under the seat, "in plain view," giving them cause to search the car. The bar, similar to the "wonder bars" used in break-ins, was accompanied by a pipe-wrench like those used to snap locks, a large screwdriver that could jimmy a window, two short socks which could be used like gloves to prevent tell-tale fingerprints and a nylon stocking large enough to slip over a head.

The officer administered the caution to the driver, who did not answer questions.

At trial, defence counsel elected to call no evidence, and the judge stated: "The Crown has proven 'possession' and 'suitability.' But where is evidence of 'intent to use?' The police did not see him, say, crossing a lawn and lurking under a window... The Section does not allow me to infer 'intent' from the absence of a reasonable explanation." Consequently, he granted a motion to dismiss.

Now, had there been a jury, and had you been a member of it, you surely would have wanted to hear from the accused. You might even have wanted to hear him say that the nylon was for his one-legged girlfriend. You might have come to think that Canadian justice is kind of odd, and that hearing this case was akin to seeing *Hamlet* without hearing a word from the principal character.

In 1995 alone, Vancouver police recorded more than 18,000 home break-ins – according to Constable Tony Arkwright the highest rate of home burglaries in Canada. They mainly occur when residents are away at work, and only about seven percent of the culprits are caught.[12] Very few of them ever come to the attention of a judge. Most B&Es are amateur affairs, with a couple of youths cruising a neighbourhood or ringing doorbells seeking a target home. These are fast get-away jobs, five or 10 minutes give or take, with the culprits long gone before the neighbours can sound an alarm. Some B&E artists specialize, going for jewelry or money that can be stuffed in pockets, or for booze, stereos and other electronic equipment that can be bundled into a pillow case. The somewhat macho culture of those who do these jobs can lead to the occasional bragging session. One young malefactor boasted to a police officer that he'd done 500 such jobs.

In the Criminal Code, the section dealing with break-in tools does not put an onus on a suspect to say what he was up to or what the tools were for – unless the suspect is found with tools *inside* the house. Outside the house – on the lawn, say – doesn't count. Too many judges look with disfavour on such "reverse onuses." Learned academics writing in law journals maintain that such onuses offend the Charter's "presumption of innocence" – something, it seems, that can easily be offended. Criminal lawyers at civil liberties meetings eloquently demand that reverse onuses receive the death penalty. And they have High Court authority to back them up.

This Hallowed Principle[13]

In 1986, the Supreme Court, soon after it went on Charter time, struck down a law that had been on the books a long time, going so far as to declare in its judgement that all reverse onuses violated a Charter section and could rarely be justified. This occurred by virtue of the *Oakes* case.

One fine spring evening in 1981, in London, Ontario, David Oakes was sitting in his parked car. The last thing on his mind was making legal history. But that was what happened, when a nosy constable ambled over and extracted from Oakes's pockets eight one-gram vials. Taking off their caps one by one, the constable's refined sense of smell detected hash oil. Oakes, quite put out, said the oil was for his personal consumption, but the worthy police officer refused to believe him and charged him with both possession and trafficking.

To be sure, the prosecution had something going for it. The Narcotics Act at that time provided that someone in possession had to present reasonably reliable evidence that the substance was not being peddled – in other words, the onus was on the accused. Oakes would not do this, on constitutional grounds, and he was cleared of the charge of peddling dope when all courts declared that such an onus was out of bounds.

Not that this was much of a case. Oakes's pockets had held eight grams, not eight kilograms, and even if both charges had stuck, he should have received much the same penalty after the judge had sized him up and taken any record into account.[14] Still, the case transformed the legal landscape. The onus on Oakes, the High Court proclaimed, conflicted with "a hallowed principle": the presumption of innocence. The judges based their reasoning on Section 11(d) of the Charter:

> "Any person charged with an offense has the right to be presumed innocent until proven guilty in a fair hearing..."

This section expresses an ancient British law. In 1606, the eminent Chief Justice Coke said, by the Common Law of England, "the decision of a court not following fair procedure is void." That, of course, raises the question of what exactly is "fair hearing"? I submit that it is one that gives a defendant his or her full say and requires the Crown to prove the whole of its case beyond reasonable doubt. And, I would add, that gets as close to the truth as possible. If a defendant does raise a reasonable doubt, the Crown will not have proven him or her guilty beyond a reasonable doubt.

There are many jurists who don't agree that putting a rebuttable inference against an accused makes the trial unfair. One was the late, great Chief Justice of Canada, Bora Laskin, who wrote (in dissent, wouldn't you know) that:

> "...while the burden of proof is always on the Crown, there is nothing wrong in putting an evidential burden on the accused to counter, on a balance of probabilities, the Crown's case."

In fact, there's no need for a doctrine that excuses a defendant from speaking for himself. If Parliament passes, as it can, a law that stamps hard on civil liberties, there are better, more direct ways for the courts to disallow it. For instance, they can hold, under Section 7 of the Charter, that the law is not consistent with "the principles of fundamental justice." Alternatively, the court could have struck down the law under which Oakes, with his eight one-gram vials of hashish, was charged. If found guilty of trafficking, he faced, at that time, a mandatory minimum seven years in jail, regardless of who he was, his record if any, or the gravity of his offence. The court should have disallowed that under Section 12, as constituting "cruel and unusual punishment." Instead, they let a hard case make bad law.

Meanwhile, the *Oakes* case has made Parliament and the Legislatures extremely nervous about enacting reverse onuses, or about defending those in place. Now such onuses can stand only if they can be found by a court to be "demonstrably justified in a free and democratic society."[15] How has this affected the lives of ordinary people? Here is an example.

In 1995, at a Vancouver intersection, a white van struck a 12-year-old boy riding his bike. The boy was reduced to a permanently vegetative state. The van belonged to one Dugan Svedic, a building contractor, and samples of paint and fibre identified it definitively as the vehicle that struck the boy. Witnesses saw the van pull away from the scene, hesitate and disappear. However, no one could identify the driver. Svedic was charged. He had given a false statement to the police. He produced witnesses who said others sometimes drove the van. But he did not take the stand.

The judge said Svedic was under no obligation to testify, and no inferences could be drawn from his refusal. Svedic was acquitted. But how did this decision serve the cause of justice? Surely, putting some onus on Svedic to say what he knew would not have violated fundamental liberties.

Hunting for a Reasonable Verdict

Now let's consider two New Brunswick deer-hunters. There was nothing unjust about the law that hauled them into court, onus or not. It was late at night when diligent game wardens spied George Macdonald and a friend in the dark woods of Charlotte County. The men had rifles. Later, the rangers saw a flash of light. They searched the men's van – no rifles, no pit lamps. But a tracking dog led them to rifles and a sealed-beam light with batteries cached in the woods.

George and his pal are charged with illegal night hunting under the Wildlife Act, which says they have something to explain. They don't. "Oh, never mind," says the judge, "this section has a reverse onus. Out it must go." Besides, no one saw them actually firing a rifle. So out, too, go the accused. As for the deer, out goes their protected-species cover.

But All, Though Complicated, is Not Lost

Some reverse onuses have managed to survive. If you try to sneak a Rolex into Canada, you must answer questions from a customs officer. If you peddle pornography, you may have to prove it has artistic merit. If you live with a prostitute, you may have to establish that you are not living off the avails of prostitution. (This may be seen as a good thing, since prostitutes are often intimidated, brutalized – even sold – by their pimps. This was held in *R v Downey*,[16] where the Court noted that Section 11(d) had been breached, but that the onus could be justified because prostitutes are often intimidated by their pimps.)

Even if not shown to be actually living with a prostitute, should not a suspected pimp, with a sleek up-market car and deluxe lifestyle, not to mention no visible means of support, have an onus to explain his income? Could that be too much to ask, knowing as we do that there is an inter-city trade in young girls who are put "on the stroll" for a few days before being whisked away to another town before some social worker closes in?

If you dine in a restaurant and take off without paying, you will be considered to have had intent to defraud, "in the absence of evidence to the contrary." And, if you've stashed recently stolen property in your basement or your car, you really have some explaining to do. From this you may conclude that the Law reveres property as much as it does silence.

You might be forgiven for thinking the Law gives us mixed signals. Luckily, some reverse onuses have not come up before the Supreme Court. There, if past judgements are anything to go by, they would be stigmatized as constitutionally accursed, but perhaps with luck let off for good behaviour.

Underlying this overwhelming and misplaced respect for the right not to explain is a feeling that forcing someone to come clean is undemocratic and unseemly – that suspects should never be put in the position of convicting themselves with words from their own mouths (though no one objects to politicians doing that).

But there are costs to consider, far beyond taxes, for a justice system that works well; for social fairness and safe neighbourhoods. These costs must be shouldered by all, including witnesses and suspects.

The Exam: An Easy Question

If you've been paying attention, Dear Reader, the following question should pose no problems, although I admit it challenges our sense of what the Law should be and do, and what "natural justice" really is. Take your time, and see if you can come up with a way to bridge the gap between moral conduct and legal practice.

- On New Year's Eve, 1997, in the small coastal community of Squamish, B.C., a doctor's son threw a party. His parents were on vacation. Some 150 young people attended. The party grew rowdy, disturbing the neighbourhood.

A popular lawyer and triathlete, Robert McIntosh, went with a friend to check his neighbour's house, as he had been asked to do. Separated from his friend in the milling throng, McIntosh found himself in an upstairs bedroom. There, encircled by a number of youths (between eight and 12, according to reports), he was beaten to death.

An RCMP investigation ensued. No fatal weapons were found. Statements were taken from some of the party attendees who had not been upstairs at the time of the beating. Some others gave false statements and refused later cooperation.

A 21-year-old logger was charged with manslaughter. But in September 1998, this charge was dropped. The officers explained they could not rely on what turned out be be misleading statements. They had encountered a "conspiracy of silence." At the time of writing, "obstruction of justice" charges are being considered, but a prosecutor now tells me, privately, that with the evidence now at hand, such charges will not likely stand up in court.

Once upon a time, before the Charter's embrace, drunk and disorderly teenagers who misled peace officers would be judged "delinquent" in youth court. Their sentences, generally, were compassionate – and hopefully salutary. A code of silence amongst friends is understandable. However, it cannot be tolerated in a democracy.

Question: One thousand words, please, on the Law as it is, and as it should be.

Chapter 6

Taking a Canadian Fifth

"Carry Master Silence to bed."

– Falstaff, in Shakespeare's *Henry the Fourth, Part II*

"No obligation" on young offenders to account for themselves and "no onus" on defendants to respond to questions – these irresponsibilities form part of the lengthening shadow of a sacred cow known as the "Right to Silence." As it now exists, this rough beast should be quickly led off to some convenient abattoir.

Silence stands arraigned before a jury of its peers, nary a lawyer among them. It is identified as a legal right to say nothing and walk on if a police officer asks you what you might know about, say, an arsenous fire. It is also identified as a right to reveal no more than your name in a paddy wagon or at a police station. Finally, if put on trial, Silence claims a right not to take the witness stand to submit to questions. (At this point, Silence is known as "the privilege against self-incrimination.")

Counts in the indictment are read:

- That Silence leaves judges and juries guessing at what the person who knows most about what happened might have to say;

- That Silence leaves reasonable men and women thinking an individual has something to hide when that person is silent in a situation where a response would naturally be expected;

- That Silence wastes the time and money of police officers and courts;

- That Silence shows too little respect for the social responsibilities that citizens all owe each other.

Before we proceed with our case, however, let us see how this legal doctrine actually works in the real world. It turns out to be rife with anomalies.

Silence Proves Illusory for Some

For some members of our criminal classes, perhaps for most, the right to silence works well enough – but not for all. Not for Rene Castellani, for one. In 1970, after two trials and appeals, he got life in prison for the slow poisoning of his wife.[1] He barely escaped the noose; lucky for him, Mrs. Castellani managed to cling to life for some months past the date on which capital punishment was abolished.

Even before his trial, Castellani was well known in the Vancouver area, where he worked as a sportscaster for radio station CKNW. In the 1960s, he began to broadcast his program from a perch at the top of a flag pole, catching the attention of fans all over B.C. Perhaps egged on by his new-found celebrity, Castellani cast aside his wife in favour of a clandestine affair with Lollie Miller, a widow 14 years his junior. Lollie pestered him for a ring, and Castellani, fatefully, decided on a divorce à la Borgia.

He bought a can of Trilox, a weed killer comprising 50 percent arsenic, and kept it under the kitchen sink. Very soon, Mrs. Castellani was complaining of gastric disorders that defied medical diagnosis. After she was admitted to hospital, her attentive husband descended from his flagpole each evening to visit her, thoughtfully bringing her delectables to supplement the hospital fare – homemade milkshakes and small bowls of sautéed ground beef (neither of which betrays the colour or scent of arsenic).

As Mrs. Castellani's health declined, her doctor's perplexity increased, eventually turning to anguish when she died. Blaming himself, he continued for weeks to pore over the nurses' notes and medical texts. Then, the light dawned

– poison had to be the cause of his patient's mysterious symptoms and agonizing death. The coroner agreed to exhume the remains for a second autopsy.

The prosecution had only the thinnest circumstantial evidence to identify Castellani as the poisoner. But the scoundrel was eventually caught out in lies to friends about his affair with Lollie, and about the trip they'd taken to Disneyland the day after he buried his wife. He'd also lied to the nurses about the food he'd brought to the hospital.

A Toronto toxicologist was called to the stand. By examining the dead woman's hair, he testified, he had established a gradual ingestion of arsenic over a three-month period. At the time of death, Mrs. Castellani's hair contained 200 times the normal amount of the toxin.

Despite this, the Crown's case was rickety, and the judge, in his discretion, left the verdict to the jury. Those worthies chose not to believe the silent Castellani. He appealed and won a re-trial. This time he took the stand, only to be subjected to a scorching cross-examination. Again the judge excoriated him and this time gave him a life sentence that stuck.

Having sampled both silence and its opposite, Castellani may have had occasion to reflect upon this time-honoured pillar of our justice system. The right to silence was designed to protect the innocent, by allowing suspects to say nothing, secure in the knowledge that their silence will prejudice neither judge nor jury. But this security can be fictitious.

In Castellani's case, his Charter Right (Section 11 [c]) "not to be compelled to be a witness…against himself " certainly proved to be deceptive. By the time of his re-trial, he was virtually compelled to take the stand, incriminating himself with his own words, since even accomplished liars find it hard to look judge and jury in the eye and hide their guilt. Indeed, in our system, mere witnesses have an easier time getting away with something. Abe Lincoln was pretty much on track when he said, "No man has a good enough memory to be a successful liar."

If the Right to Silence was but a chimera for Castellani, for most culprits it is not. Uncounted numbers are not charged because they need not give an account of their activities. Others who are charged can find in silence the key to freedom. Consider Neil Hebert, who kindly lent his name to a case that has become a leading precedent.[2]

A Robber Walks

Armed robbery was not Neil Hebert's regular calling. It was simply a handy method of occasionally raising needed cash. That was the case on January 11, 1987, in Whitehorse, when Hebert donned a ski mask, entered the Klondike Inn and brandished a claw hammer at the frightened clerk. After scooping $180 from the till, Hebert warned the clerk to give him 10 minutes before calling the Mounties, then fled on foot.

Three months later, the Mounties got their man in the lounge of the Taku Hotel, thanks to informers' tips. (Of course, such tips are not evidence.) At the lock-up, Hebert duly responded to the caution with the incantation, "Won't say anything until I see a lawyer." A lawyer was called, and Hebert was assigned a cell with another inmate whom he took to be a soulmate-in-crime. Soon they were confiding to each other their low opinions of cops in general, and in no time at all, Hebert was telling his new pal about his recent hit. The cellmate, of course, was a disguised police mole wearing a body pack. Herbert had been well and truly stung. Thanks to his loose lips, the RCMP now had enough evidence to go to a jury.

The case wound its way through the legal system, eventually reaching the Supreme Court, which overturned the Court of Appeal ruling and threw out Hebert's true confession. In doing so, the Court propped up its idol, Silence, with three legal pronouncements. All three were to proliferate, spelling trouble as they give birth to their own precedents.

Cellmate Confidential

Justice John Sopinka, in the core judgement, made these points:

First, the Learned Judge asked himself: "Can jail-house confessions induced by deception withstand Charter scrutiny?" His answer, an unalloyed negative, upset several centuries of common-law jurisprudence, which traditionally held such confessions admissible if deemed "reliable." (Unreliable confessions included those beaten out of an accused or purchased with a promise.) Back in 1970, in *R v Wray* (1970, CCC 1 (SCC)), the High Court had said that "a court has no discretion to exclude voluntary, truthful statements."

Ironically, the Supreme Court would have accepted a confession from Hebert if the police had deceptively wire-tapped him telling all to a genuine con or to a visitor.

In this case, however, with a few strokes of a pen, Justice Sopinka opened up a rich vein of judicial ore. When, if ever, were admissions to undercover officers (or their agents) evidence? This question will keep lawyers and courts busy for decades. Indeed, since the Hebert case, disguised police moles must follow rules as complicated as medieval courtship rites. They cannot dress up like prison padres; they are forbidden to employ alcohol; they must try not to lie to their suspects (apart from their appearance); and they must not actively elicit admissions. All that is left to them is the role of passive listener.

This reasoning has stripped away a key investigatory device and given freedom to Albert Brown, an Alberta murderer who, among others, did not deserve it.

In 1991, Brown, a rejected husband, killed his former wife's boyfriend. But he couldn't keep his lip zippered – before the murder, he had been heard swearing vengeance. He had also been seen with the victim on the fatal night and had even called his ex-wife the next morning to say, "Now I can forgive you."

A clever undercover officer was planted in Brown's cell. He told our Albert how he had beaten a murder rap once himself, and how he had a friend who was dying of cancer and who just might take the fall for Brown. Our man soon spilled the beans.

Later, at trial, with legal advice, Brown signed a waiver, allowing his voluntary admissions to be used as evidence against him. His lawyer can't be blamed for this; after all, he was merely following the law as it then was. In the 1981 *Rothman* case,[3] the Supreme Court had ruled that confessions stood unless that had been "induced by fear of prejudice or hope of advantage." Brown was convicted of first-degree murder.

Then, from on high, like Manna from heaven, came the *Hebert* judgement. Brown's lawyer, not one to miss a chance, argued in the appeal court that his client's cell words should be blotted out. "You're too late to raise that," said the court.

But not the Supreme Court, ordering a re-trial for Brown.[4] At the new trial, the judge was to decide whether Brown had known the imposter was really a policeman. If he had known, his confession would stick. If he had not, his words would be inadmissible.

We should approach such a conundrum gingerly. Close attention to reasoning such as this can be harmful to one's brain. Surely if Brown had known his cellmate was a cop he'd have kept mum. And knowing or not, the jury should have heard the whole recording to help it decide whether his admissions were trustworthy.

When "Fair" is Not Fair

Now back to *Hebert*. Justice Sopinka next declared that the right to silence was "an integral part of an accused's right to a fair trial," basing his conclusion on Section 7, the "fair trial" section of the Charter. This section, however, is silent on Silence. In any event, simple horse-sense suggests that a trial in which an accused has a duty to explain himself ought to be considered fair.

Justice Sopinka's rationale in rejecting Hebert's admission was, of course, that doing otherwise would bring justice into disrepute. Once more, the sagacious pleas of judges in the lower reaches of the system were passed over – for one, Ontario Justice Zuber who, in the *Duguay* case (cited in Chapter 1) said that, before tossing out key evidence, the court should have a thought for the plight of the crime victim.

After all, the Charter's "fair trial" section says that "everyone" is entitled to them. That night clerk who was terrorized by Hebert at the Klondike Inn; Albert Brown's slain ex-wife; the public – most Canadians would readily agree that trials shorn of believable evidence are decidedly *not* fair.

Even convicted souls have a grudging respect for the Law if the courts treat them fairly. Never mind that old saw, "No man ere felt the halter draw with good opinion of the law." Canadians up on a charge, be it a petty one or a grave one, feel better for the verdict if they are accorded substantive, meaningful rights and an open and impartial tribunal; the right to confront, question and rebut adverse witnesses; a jury, if the charge is serious; and the high onus on the Crown to prove its case beyond a reasonable doubt. Those are some of the values that really matter. But throwing out good evidence? Few respect the law for that.

Hebert may have had a fair trial. It was his fellow citizens who did not.

In the light of this, let's consider the trial of a randy Toronto police officer. His superiors charged him with attempting to purchase the sexual services of an underage 17-year-old prostitute. He told them (with no lawyer at his side, and despite the fact that he had been seen meeting her) that he had not even been at Queen Street and Bathurst, and that he hadn't met the young woman in question.

At his trial, he came up with a different story when the Crown attorney, naturally, wanted to cross-examine him to test his credibility. "No way," intoned our High Court, where this case had somehow ended up. One story got him off; a jury hearing both stories would have done him in.[5] Oh, worshipful Silence, how thy shadow lengthens!

Not that this was a heinous offence – save for the law it made. Sinners commonly lie about sexual misadventures. Presidents and politicians, too, may fib. I can recall one MP who was holding forth vehemently to a colleague in the parliamentary restaurant in Ottawa, only to be interrupted with, "You're lying!" "I know," replied the MP heatedly. "But hear me out."

Think Nothing of It

Now for the third prong of the *Hebert* case. The Court went on to provide the right to silence with more protective clothing. In its words, "Even if the circumstances cry out for an explanation to a person in authority, silence cannot support an inference of guilt."

Now, I think you will agree that here, with all due respect, Justice Sopinka takes an extraordinary departure from the wisdom of everyday life, not to mention a departure from literary wisdom. In 1687, the poet John Dryden wrote (in *The Hind and The Panther*) that "secret guilt by silence is betrayed." What would any "reasonable person" make of this? Consider the implications. A card cheat introduces a marked deck into a poker game. The losers, spotting it, are bound to put two and two together if the cheater doesn't volunteer the information about how he came by the deck. Or a boy goes missing from a summer camp. Surely the counsellor in whose charge he was will be expected to say where and when he last saw the boy – unless, illogically, he is asked by a police officer who suspects foul play. Then everyone is expected to pay no heed to his not answering. However, this is hard to do. That silence equals guilt is embedded in our human psyche.

Did the Charter force the Court in *Hebert* to rule that "silence cannot support an inference of guilt"? Most emphatically it did not. Section 11(e) of the document sets out the right of an accused on trial not to be compelled to testify. But that's all it says. It does not indicate what a judge or jury may make of an accused's failure to try to clear himself.

Let's say a woman is mugged and robbed. The accused denies he was involved. But the woman had caught a glimpse of a mermaid tattooed on her attacker's right bicep. She tells this to the jury. The accused does not take the stand or bare his arm. What jury in its right mind wouldn't take that as an "inference of guilt" – even though neither judge nor prosecution can make any comment about it.

The *Hebert* case put the Law on the wrong side of the looking glass, transporting it into the realm of fancy. The High Court did step back, but only a little, in 1994, by saying it was lawful for jurors to draw an adverse inference from the failure of an accused to testify. Indeed, it is hard to imagine how they could be prevented from doing so.[6]

You have to wonder if judges really worship the idol Silence as faithfully as they let on. They have decided[7] that, though the police have to tell a suspect that "anything you say can be used against you," they don't have to tell him that "your silence cannot be used against you." Why? Because they don't believe it? Or because they really want him to talk? Whatever the reason, the caution denies an informed choice to run-of-the-mill suspects, while smart crooks already know as much about silence as the police do.

The Origins of Silence

You may be wondering how a right not to co-operate, rather than a duty to do so, came to play a leading role in our criminal laws. Read on.

Our laws slowly emerged from the womb of time. They began as whims, superstitions, moralities, customs and expediencies and were first engraved in the Code of Hammurabi, King of Babylon, in the 18th century B.C. Much later, the Greek and Roman traditions were encoded by the Byzantine emperor Justinian in the sixth century A.D. These "laws" permeated English common law as the King's judges handed down verdicts, later comparing notes at dinner in London's Inns of Court, and getting their decisions written up.

On top of this foundation came various great charters – the Magna Carta of 1215, the Bill of Rights of 1689. As the law developed, its humane aspects grew – though not without setbacks, such as the reign of the Star Chamber, which was abolished in 1641. There, confessions were pressed from guilty and innocent alike, they "having first been shown the instruments of their torture."

In reaction to extorted confessions, a statute of 1846 allowed the accused to refuse to answer authorities' questions, and statements not made "voluntarily" – "without fear of prejudice or promise of reward"– were ruled out. Finally, in 1898, a statute was created to permit the accused to take the stand and testify in his own defence.

However, the right to silence did not find a place in this evolution without serious debate. Its opponents included the noted Utilitarian philosopher Jeremy Bentham, who wrote in 1827 that this "right" would be "the first demand if all criminals assembled and framed a system after their own wishes."[8] Bentham also stated that "innocence never takes advantage of it, while guilt invokes the privilege of silence."

Silence in the Courts!

With Bentham's words ringing in his ears, Silence, in his court appearances, is giving spotty and uneven performances. Among them:

- Three young men sit under arrest in the back seat of a police cruiser in Scarborough, Ontario. Two are talkative. "Yeah, we saw this Morris behind Arnie's Sales, keys in the ignition, got in and went for a ride, hit the gas when we saw you guys." The third keeps his trap shut, eventually pleading "not guilty" and at trial, serving up an alibi to the judge. "I wasn't with them when they took the car – I didn't know it was stolen."

    Neither the prosecutor nor judge can ask him, "Why didn't you say that when your friends were tying you into the theft?" Nor could the court consider his failure to exculpate himself when he was being inculpated.

    Result? The talkative two end up with a record. The third is saved by his pregnant silence.[9] By the way, the silent one's lawyer had presented the police with a letter saying he was not to be questioned. This has become a typical routine, to try to ensure that Silence is not heard.

- A nurse is found in a pool of blood in her Vancouver apartment. Her husband says only that "I was out running errands and came back to find her murdered." His lawyer informs the police: "He will continue to exercise his right to silence." Stymied, anxious officers and grieving family members call for an inquest, hoping the husband can be made to talk. Although almost unheard of in murder cases, a coroner's jury is summoned.

The husband admits to the jury that he had lied about her wedding ring. It could not have been lost in Florida, as he had previously said, since it was found tucked into a sofa on which he had sat while attending the police station. Still, the inquest did not find enough evidence to justify a prosecutor sending the man to trial. Later, the coroner – no friend of Silence – exclaims to a newspaper reporter, "What if he had testified, 'I did it,' or words to that effect? That admission couldn't have been used against him" under Section 5 of The Canada Evidence Act, a branch of Silence's family. "That would have given the justice system a black eye." The police file remains open.[10]

Justice Twaddle Speaks Up

In 1989, a judge with the disarming name of Twaddle, A. K., of the Manitoba Court of Appeal, broke with conventional legal wisdom. Bravely, he ventured the view that "the Charter did not abrogate the rule of common sense." In the case to which he referred, the social stakes were high. A man was charged with brutal and repeated sexual assaults on his step-daughter while she was between seven and 11 years old. She testified and was believed by the trial judge. However, she had no witness who saw her bruises and vaginal bleeding; nor did anyone support her reasons for running away from home at age 12.

Now, bear in mind the long-standing legal maxim that states that it is dangerous, in such cases, to convict on the uncorroborated evidence of the complainant. The accused had not taken the stand. Nevertheless, he was convicted, and his appeal was to no avail.

"The trial judge," Justice Twaddle wrote, "did believe her, and this Court can take into account his failure to take the stand and contradict her story." This independent stance tore a hole in Silence's protective clothing.[11] It was a two-to-one decision, with J. F. O'Sullivan, J.A., dissenting, arguing that "no comment can be allowed on failure to testify."

Another tear was to appear shortly afterwards, when two young men pulled a break-and-enter at a stereo store in Scarborough, Ontario. The wily prosecutor decided to proceed against them with separate trials for the same offence. Each was compelled to testify as a witness against his accomplice. Prosecutorial discretion took an end run around Silence – and got away with it.[12] Did the Court say this dodge had brought Justice into disrepute? No.

Then, two cousins were tried together for the murder and robbery of a man they "befriended" at a bar in Belleville, Ontario. Each tried the "cutthroat" defence – the first, when he was picked up, blamed the other for the killing, but did not testify at trial. The second did take the stand, at that point laying the blame on his cousin. Cross-examined by the other's lawyer, he was asked, "Why should we believe you now, when you didn't say that when you were arrested?" The Supreme Court held that an opposing defence counsel could ask that question, provided the jury was told it went to credibility and not to proof of guilt. (Why can't the same liberty be granted to the prosecution in such instances?) Justice Beverley McLachlin was the lone dissenter, saying: "Any faulting of an accused for exercising the right to silence effectively puts an end to that right."[13]

But the end is nowhere near. Dysfunctional Silence continues to sow dissension among judges. Recently, a rankling debate surfaced in the Law Reports between the late Justice Sopinka and the Chief Justice. It was on a question that won't go away, at least as long as Silence reigns: "When, if ever, can a judge comment on, or consider, or even contemplate, the silence of an accused that cries out for explanation?" The majority answer of Justice Sopinka (by five to four) was "Practically never."

So, in a 1997 trial, a decision came down that made no sense. A building manager had come upon two young men using a screwdriver, trying to break into a car in the parking lot. Challenged, one claimed to have no ID, while the other produced an expired driver's licence with a photo bearing some resemblance. He was charged. A trial judge, without a jury, took notice of his failure to testify in finding proof beyond a reasonable doubt. Both the B.C. Appeal Court and the Supreme Court said he couldn't include that failure, even with other evidence falling just short of proof.[14] Silence chalked up another victory, though it was a close call, with an assist from his friend Nonsensical.

Witnesses Must Bear Witness

Is it not odd that our law doesn't insist that criminal suspects answer questions, while innocent witnesses have to say everything they know about the crime? Witnesses undergo more than inconvenience. They must speak up in open court and face what can be the ordeal of cross-examination. Some might have to concede they spent the night with another fellow's wife. Indeed, one Alberta witness in a poisoning trial had to admit, to his chagrin, that he had offered the accused $2 million to be his mistress for 10 years. Others, though protected, have to incriminate themselves publicly. Their testimony could lose them friends and expose them to retaliation by the accused's allies. Nevertheless, most of them do their duty, some because they must, but most from a sense of civic obligation.

All witnesses can be compelled to take the stand – except husbands and wives against each other, or lawyers and clients as to what passed between them. Journalists can be made to reveal their sources; priests to say what was confessed. Sexual-assault counsellors and psychologists, though they themselves be white as snow, must speak up – unless, black as hell, they are the accused.

In one instance, an expert had to give his opinion all over again for free. His client had won a re-trial but run out of money. The expert complained in vain.

The old British Common Law required citizens to do more than simply testify. It obliged them, morally as well as legally, to actively assist in the suppression of crime. Until our century, "it was a felony silently to observe the commission of a crime without using every endeavour to apprehend the offender; and discover the crime to a magistrate." [15] How that duty has faded! Today, rights trump responsibilities.

A prime example is the case of the woman who was sexually assaulted in a hotel room in Surrey, B.C. Gino Odjick, a hockey player for the Vancouver Canucks, had been in the room but left, leaving her with a friend of his, before the alleged assault. Odjick refused to tell the police who his friend was. His lawyer – like all his ilk considered to be an "officer of the court" – was quoted as saying that he "saw no reason why Odjick should cooperate with the police." [16] Legally, bizarre as it may seem, Odjick didn't have to cooperate, since doing so might have landed him in trouble as an accomplice. Hence, no charges ensued.

South of the 49th Parallel the trial of Timothy McVeigh for the murder of 168 people in the Oklahoma City bombing was a grand spectacular, grist for the media. One witness has said he saw McVeigh at a Ryder rental outlet picking up the truck that carried the explosive mix, in company with an unidentifiable "John Doe." It would, of course, have been a waste of breath for investigators, at any time, to have asked McVeigh to answer a simple, "Were you there? If so, who was with you? If not, where were you that day?" Forget such questions. Silence bars the way to an answer, whether true or false, contradictable or not.

Was there a broader conspiracy in the McVeigh case? McVeigh's attorney hinted that there was. But the American (and Canadian) criminal justice system can't get close to uncovering it, even though it allowed McVeigh's lawyer to accuse the FBI of scapegoating his client by holding back on evidence by not producing John Doe.

The late, notable American judge, Benjamin Cardozo, would not have been upset had those questions been put to McVeigh, his answers checked out or his silence deemed suspicious. Cardozo once wrote:

"Justice would not perish if the accused were subject to orderly inquiry."[17]

False Friend of the Innocent

Some who object to "orderly inquiry" maintain that silence helps to shield the innocent from conviction. Of course, Voltaire was quite right when he wrote, "It is better to risk saving a guilty person than to condemn an innocent one."[18] But the sad truth of the matter is that the innocent are more likely to be convicted if they fail to account for their activities. Silence breeds suspicion.

David Milgaard's name may spring to mind in this context. In 1970, young Milgaard was sentenced to life in prison for the sex slaying of a Saskatoon woman. Milgaard did not testify at his trial. He was found guilty and served 22 years in prison. He was released only after the Supreme Court, on a special referral, found doubt in his conviction.[19] The Supreme Court did not suggest that Milgaard should have sworn to his innocence at his trial. But, were he innocent, taking the stand could hardly have harmed him.

Incidentally, during the Supreme Court hearing of the Milgaard conviction, the Chief Justice was himself extremely disrespectful of Silence. One

Larry Fisher, a sexual predator who might have done the killing for which Milgaard was wrongly accused, was summoned into the box. From the Bench, the Chief Justice fixed on him his glittering eye and subjected him to a withering cross-examination as to his possible culpability. It was all on TV. But the Chief's own court wouldn't think of letting trial judges carry on like that.

True, some defendants have a good reason for not taking the stand – perhaps a criminal record they don't want brought out in cross-examination. But a record may fairly bear on credibility; if it does not, the judge will stop such inquiries. Juries should be trusted to assess the believability of all those giving evidence, under the careful instructions of the judge. Even a "hopeless," but innocent, accused should testify. His or her testimony may be given haltingly, with some memory lapses and inconsistencies. But it will have the ring of truth. Judges and juries are more likely to disbelieve slick, well-rehearsed, an-answer-to-everything performances.

Juries hate being kept in the dark about the kind of person they are trying. In London, England, a man was up for sexual assault upon two prostitutes. His Q.C. subjected the ladies of the night to scorching cross-examination, painting them as without morality or conscience, pursuing a vendetta against his client. The accused got off without taking the box. Later the jurors learned, to their dismay, that he had spent a year in jail for a previous vicious assault, holding a knife to his victim's throat in a van complete with straps and a mattress.

Where Silence is not Golden

Canada has what Justice Sopinka has called "an accusatorial and adversarial system of justice."[20] But this is not true of the administration of justice in many Western European countries, which were founded on the principles of Roman law. They are, nonetheless, free and democratic societies. Look at Switzerland. In that country, one Cyril Belshaw, a University of B.C. professor, was indicted for the murder of his wife, Betty. The Belshaws had been staying in Switzerland at their holiday home, although Cyril claimed he was in Paris when Betty went missing. Her body was eventually found, wrapped in a plastic garbage bag.

After Cyril returned to Vancouver, the Swiss authorities asked the RCMP to question him about his wife's disappearance. Well-versed in his legal rights, he refused to cooperate – although he did confuse the Swiss police in the identification of his wife's remains by sending them fabricated dental records. Later, incautiously, Cyril attended a conference in France. There his arrest warrant was executed, and he was extradited to Switzerland.

Under Swiss law, anyone involved in a serious crime, even as a witness, is promptly and thoroughly questioned, under oath, by a Magistrate in open court. Legal counsel may appear with the suspect or witness at the examination – to make sure the questions are understood, to clear up any ambiguities in the responses and to object to any tricks or bullying. If a suspect has already made damaging admissions, the suspect is asked to repeat, deny or explain them. The proceedings are videotaped. Failure of someone under suspicion to respond fully and candidly is viewed as an indication of guilty participation.

Belshaw was examined, with those safeguards, and his answers led to further investigation. At his later trial, which lasted all of two days, the jury found the murder charge "Not Proven," a distinction which is made under Swiss law from "Not Guilty." He returned to Canada a free man, but only after paying a fine for altering his wife's dental records.

Great Britain – the cradle of civil liberties and home of the Mother of Parliaments – also now manages to dispense justice without allowing a blanket right to silence. The British courts have been gradually restricting this "right" since 1988, when Parliament curbed the right to silence of suspected terrorists in Northern Ireland. This was considered a special case, since terrorists are usually trained to withstand interrogation without betraying themselves or their allies.

Then, in 1990, Parliament required that company officers in inquiries involving serious fraud must respond to official questions and reveal all pertinent records. This, too, was regarded as a special case, for such frauds can bilk ordinary people of billions and are easily concealed in a complex web of false invoices, "gentlemen's agreements" and so on.

Finally, in the fall of 1994, Britain enacted a new form of "caution" to be read to all detained under suspicion. It replaced the old "You need not answer, but anything you say may be held against you" with a new phrase that goes:

> "You do not have to say anything. But if you do not mention now something you later use in your defence, the Court may decide that your failure to mention it now strengthens the case against you."

Great Britain has also made it expensive to remain silent when on trial. A refusal to testify may allow "inferences contrary to the interests of the accused to be drawn."

A few years ago, we Canadians gazed south, appalled and fascinated, at the trial of O. J. Simpson for murdering his wife, Nicole Brown. As the months wore on, we saw the truth sustaining grievous casualties, and time and money thrown to the winds like so much confetti. From the beginning, O.J.'s defence team put everyone else on trial: the victim and her surviving relatives and friends; the police; the coroner; the witnesses; and even, briefly, the judge himself. As for O.J., he didn't say a word – about the knife he bought, the scratches on his body, the gloves. The name of the game was not truth-seeking, but victory at any cost.

Later, of course, Brown's family sued O.J., and a jury found him responsible for the murder, although he still denies it. Another American who managed to get off on a charge of murdering his wife did a post-trial radio talk show. Asked by the host, "But *did* you kill her?" he responded, "My position is 'no.'"

Never in Canada?

Many Canadians deny that an O.J.-style trial could happen here. But they are sadly misinformed. Too much of this type of justice is already occurring, and our laws on silence play a major role in spinning out trials, clogging courtrooms, bloating costs and complicating criminal investigations.

The serious rape-murders enacted by Paul Bernardo and Karla Homolka offer a prime example. Perhaps the lives of the young women tortured by this unholy pair would have been saved if peace officers had had more authority to question in depth possible perpetrators. Perhaps the truth would have been better served if, following Bernardo's arrest, his defence lawyer had had to disclose details of his presentation. After all, the Crown must disclose its material to the defence.

Suppose, as with a civil case, Bernardo had had to face an examination for discovery (a pre-trial hearing) soon after his arrest. If he were to be sued for damages by a victim's family, he would have to answer questions in such a hearing or else be in contempt of court.

In Sweden, after a serious crime, possible witnesses have a duty to stay with the police for up to six hours – and a suspect up to 12 hours – for examination. They may have counsel with them, and names are not published at this stage. Under rules like these, Bernardo would have been examined as a stalking and rape suspect in an earlier Scarborough investigation.

Of course, the consequences in a criminal trial can be far more severe that those in a civil suit, and the burden of proof on the Crown is therefore much heavier. But no one has ever claimed that pre-trial discoveries dilute a civil trial's fairness.

On a point of lesser importance, Bernardo's legal-aid bills – bills ultimately footed by the taxpayer – ran to more than $1 million. While it's difficult to put a price on justice, balance sheets are about fair choices and moral priorities. In 1994, Mr. Justice Doherty, an Ontario appeals court judge, rejected the cost-benefit approach to justice. He wrote: "Fairness cannot ultimately be measured in a balance sheet." (*R v Parks,* 1994, 24 CR (4th) 81 at 110.)

But of course financial resources *are* a factor. Money saved by shortening drawn-out cases could lower the national deficit or create jobs for troubled young people, something that could, ultimately, have a salutary effect on the crime rate.

Indeed, estimates suggest that the 1998 trial of Albert Walker, a Canadian businessman found guilty of murdering Ronald Platt, a man whose identity he had assumed three years earlier, which took 11 days in Britain, might have lasted six weeks in Canada. University of Ottawa law professor David Paciocco explained this by saying there is a different "legal culture" in Canada that produces longer trials. Paciocco added that English judges also seem to have a more "no-nonsense" attitude than their Canadian counterparts.

Alan Gold, a Toronto criminal lawyer, agreed. "If you look at how long trials take, the United States is at one end of the spectrum, Britain is at the other and Canada falls in between," said Gold, president of the Criminal Lawyers' Association. He added that prosecutors in British trials, who are always senior barristers, are more professional and less likely to seek to enter marginal evidence.

The length of trials for serious crimes in Canada has probably doubled or even tripled in the last 20 years, says Edmonton lawyer Marvin Bloom. Thanks to the impact of the Charter of Rights and Freedoms, there are now often lengthy trials within a trial in Canada, wherein lawyers argue about the admissibility of evidence or counselling records of sexual-assault complainants.[21]

A Matter of Common Sense

Now to the main count in this indictment, that Silence has scant regard for the interests of Society.

I submit that the genius of British common law is its ability constantly to adapt to changing circumstances. But while that law continues to evolve in other jurisdictions, in Canada and the United States it remains mired in outworn conventions and practices.

In contrast, Singapore, albeit far too tightly managed for our taste, bases its trial processes on British common law principles and its constitution (similar to our own Charter) mandates fair hearings. Moreover, it retains as a final court of appeal the Judicial Committee of the House of Lords sitting in London.

In 1980, one Haw Tua Tau stood trial in a Singapore court charged with the murder of two persons. No witness placed him at the crime scene. The only evidence the Crown presented was that Haw's trousers were stained with mud and cartridge residue, and that he was not at home at the time of the crime. Procedural rules required him to proffer a reasonable explanation. When he failed to do so, Haw was convicted.

His appeal reached the British Law Lords. Speaking for them, Lord Diplock affirmed that the common law principles of natural justice must apply. He went on to say, however, that the Crown's evidence, though insufficient to convict, was nonetheless a case to meet; and further:

> "It calls for an explanation, if one exists...and failure to give an explanation may, as a matter of common sense, allow an inference that there is no explanation and that the accused is guilty."

Here, the Law Lords struck a modern balance between an individual's expectations and personal choice, and the duty he or she owes to the community. That balance should reflect civilized traditions derived from the Judeo-Christian tradition, the Greek notion of *civitas,* and the more recent influence of social democracy.

But legal establishments, like most professions, shy away from change. Lawyers and judges develop a cast of mind shaped by their training and daily work. The French call this *déformation professional;* others might call it tunnel vision. Whatever the label we use, it means all Canadians must do their part if we are to get meaningful law reform.

An Appeal to Citizen Jurors

What's so great about a right to silence that shelters defendants while they figure out what to say? It could be, "I wasn't even near the murder scene"; or, if spotted there, "I was there but didn't do the stabbing"; or, "I did it in self-defence"; or, "I did it, but I had a legally sanctioned psychological reason for acting as I did." Who can be proud of a system that lets that go on? Or a system that lets crime-control slip and slip?

Take the case of a Toronto police agent, one Ms. Eva Mead, who went missing for a day. Officers tried in vain to contact her. Fearful for her safety, without much to go on, they brought in Richard Babinski on a charge of breaking and entering her apartment. They neglected to read him his rights, and – not wanting some accomplice to kill Mead to keep her quiet – tried to prevent word of his arrest from leaking out.

For two hours, Babinski bucked questions about her whereabouts. Then a sergeant came in and asked, "Richard, where's Eva?" He replied, "You made me phone her. You figure it out. Talk to my lawyer." She had already been killed – but who can blame police for trying to save her? The Supreme Court, later on, blamed them – in a way – by ruling out Babinski's words at his murder trial, although one dissenting justice, Madam L'Heureux Dubé, did not.[22]

Let's forget for a moment murderers, rapists and robbers. Let's think about people who set fires. The Canadian Insurance Bureau says we have about 13,000 arson frauds each year, costing some $500 million in insurance pay-outs. "Thrill" arsonists usually give themselves away in time; "revenge" arsonists are a little easier to catch. But it's not easy to bring the fraudsters to justice. It does not help that the Law offers anyone who knows anything about a fire the right to silence.

Or what about a ring of car thieves that places officers' lives at risk in a high-speed chase. Conscientious officers want respect for reasonable methods of law enforcement. It is the absence of procedures for orderly, civil but thorough inquiries into crime that leads to more coercive, abusive police tactics. No wonder peace officers feel frustrated in their work. Not surprisingly, some try to find ways to get over, under or around the right to silence. What's that do for the Law's repute?

When there's been serious mischief – if a child is missing, perhaps abducted; if armed hold-up men are on the loose, ready to fire with little to lose – what's so wrong about bringing suspects before a justice of the peace and asking them to tell what they know about it?

In a civil, formal interrogation, recorded in audio and video, many baddies will lie, or try to, or concoct a tale to outsmart the police or to protect someone. But get away with it? Not likely – especially without rehearsal time and forced to look a JP in the eye while answering detailed questions that will be matched with verifiable facts. Instead, we put no price tag on refusing to cooperate. How long can civilization stand that?

We come into this world with freedoms to enjoy – precious ones. But we are born with some conditions precedent – responsibilities to others, which we must honour from time to time. What's so great in a democracy about a right not to cooperate with those who've been chosen to promote public safety? Do we have a right to run and hide?

The Quiz

Has your attention been wandering, Dear Reader? Here's a short test of your understanding, not to mention your patience.

- An unknown voice is taped during hostage-taking negotiations. Later, the accused uses the same voice when he testifies at a taped *voir dire* (a hearing within his trial, from which the jury is barred, to decide what it should hear). Could the tape be used in the main trial? Not likely! An officer listened over and over to the two tapes and wanted to tell the jury that it was the same voice. No way, ruled the court – that would be like the accused incriminating himself.[23]

  Write a treatise explaining why a voice is entitled to the right to silence.

- A court decides that a suspect is not obliged to enter an ID line-up, although a witness was able to pick his photo out from amongst others.[24]

  Explain why line-ups offend the Charter, addressing this conundrum: Is body language entitled to silence?

- Police resort to a ruse to catch a criminal, falsely telling the suspect that they have proof of her guilt – whereupon she says, "I might be able to get the stolen goods," and does get them. At her trial, the judge blows the whistle, saying it wasn't fair to get the goods on her that way.[25]

Fair or foul? Discuss.

Chapter 7

Paying Too Much for Privacy

"It is a melancholy reflection that Liberty shall be equally exposed to danger, whether the Government have too much or too little power."
– James Madison, writing to Thomas Jefferson, 1787

Search as you might, the word "privacy" does not appear anywhere in Canada's Charter. Nevertheless, its meaning pervades every page of that document, as much a part of it as the paper it is printed on. Louis Brandeis, late of the U.S. Supreme Court, called privacy "the right to be left alone." It is a value that fosters individual creativity and an inner life, permitting us to be masters or mistresses of our own bodies and thoughts.

Thanks to this concept, you don't have to allow your sins, venial or mortal, to be splashed all over the front page of a tabloid for no good reason. Your employer can't install a hidden camera in the restroom – at least, unless pilfering is probably rife. Your shopping habits can't be digitalized and retailed to advertisers seeking soft targets. Nosy neighbours must keep their distance, Peeping Toms must be jailed and police officers must not barge into our lives, homes and belongings without lawful and rational justification.

Search and seizure must be justified by the times, places and facts, where the degree of the intrusion is balanced against the public's need for social safety. There must be an understanding that civil liberties can only flourish in an orderly society.

It's unlikely that Ruby Collins, who was quietly quaffing a beer in a pub in Gibsons, B.C., one evening in 1982, was thinking about her right to privacy when Constable John Woods, a drug-squad narc, pounced on her. Shouting "Police," he applied a choke-hold to Collins's throat and snatched something from her clenched hand. It was a small green balloon, bulging with heroin.

Five years later, in the Supreme Court of Canada, Woods was chastised for invading Ruby's right to privacy. His search and seizure, he learned, had been "unreasonable" – so unreasonable that the evidence of the heroin was tossed out, and the Crown's case against Collins with it.[1]

Now, suppose you are a member of some higher appellate tribunal. Once you've assuaged your appetite for details, you will be asked which judgement was more reasonable: the on-the-spot decision of Constable Woods, or the reserved judgement of the Court?

You will discover this valued human right – the individual's prerogative to be left alone and free from unwanted public attention – conflicts with citizens' right to a fair measure of security against harmful activities. And you will hear me argue that the Collins decision put too big a crimp in the ability of peace officers to protect the public. You will also hear me argue that those judges who faulted Constable Woods for acting unreasonably used the wrong test.

Consider Section 8 of the Charter, the privacy section:

"Everyone has the right to be secure against unreasonable search or seizure."

Ah, but whose opinion counts as to what is "unreasonable?" Our laws had long and sensibly held that it is not the opinion of the police officer that counts, nor that of the law professor, nor that of the judge. Instead, the law insists that we look to "the ordinary reasonable man, the man on the Clapham omnibus," to use Lord Justice Bowen's much-quoted dictum, in *McQuire v Western Morning News* ([1903] 2 KB 108 at 109), for a sense of what is "reasonable" under various laws.

By this measure, I submit, the judges were wrong in viewing Woods's conduct through their own eyes and appraising it in the light of their own private values and refined legal concepts. They should have been representing what they discerned to be the informed and conscientious opinion of a responsible citizen. Their error led to dangerous consequences.

But back to Constable Woods, and the particulars of why he pounced as he did.

Woods and his partner had been asked to come to Gibsons, a coastal village not far from Vancouver, by the local RCMP detachment. The chief had said the town had a heroin problem. So the two officers arrived, did some surveillance, and then took in whatever gossip they could pick up. (Much later, some of it would be wrongly excluded from court evidence.) Suitably disguised in jeans and sweatshirts, they hung out for a while at the Cedars Pub, where they spied Ruby and her husband sitting at a table with another man and woman.

When the two men left, the officers tailed them to a nearby trailer park. There, they interrupted a narcotics sale, booked the two men and seized heroin from their car, along with drug paraphernalia. The officers then went back to the pub, since Constable Woods was now nurturing a suspicion that Ruby was holding more H for her husband. His experience and his nose for evidence told him that he was on no trifling mission. After all, heroin can find its way onto school playgrounds.

Ruby and the other woman were now sitting at a different table. As we have seen, Constable Woods, suspicious but not sure, moved quickly, taking Ruby by the throat to prevent her from swallowing any evidence. And he did find heroin in her hand.

A needlessly brutal search would clearly have been "unreasonable." But the Court did not fault Woods for using excessive force, nor for his use of the choke-hold. The Law accepts that drugs for sale are often carried in condoms or capsules in the mouth for quick passage to the bowels, should the cops show up. Woods had to act decisively, or not at all.

The Court did not doubt that Woods acted in "good faith" in discharging his duties as he saw them. Nothing suggested that his behaviour had been actuated by bias or any other ulterior motive or that he had been cavalier or contemptuous of Ruby's Charter rights.

Nevertheless, the Court gave Woods no credit for finding incriminating evidence in Ruby's possession. That was held to be irrelevant: it didn't bear on whether he had "probable cause" before he made his move. This may be logical, in the strictest sense of that word, but the Law should be wary of its friend Logic. Woods had acted intuitively, drawing on his experience as a narcotics enforcement officer. Surely the Court should have taken that into consideration in deciding if his search had been reasonable. "The life of the Law," said the late U.S. Chief Justice Oliver Wendell Holmes, Jr., "is not logic but experience."

Sadly, the Court ignored Holmes's wise words, ruling that Woods's suspicions, even in the circumstances described, did not amount to "reasonable cause." It thereby proceeded to "disassociate" itself from Woods's conduct, to quote from the ruling, by suppressing the evidence of Ruby's stash of H. Had it not done so, it opined, the administration of justice might have been brought into "disrepute," as set out in the Charter's Section 24 (2).

The Court did say that the gossip Woods had picked up should have been admitted in evidence to shore up his grounds to search Ruby. As it was ruled out by the trial judge, it earned Ruby a re-trial. But however he came to be in the Cedars Pub, what Woods saw fully justified his search. After all, Ruby had been sitting with people found to be trading in drugs. Her husband had been arrested. She had, as it turned out, more than just a capsule or two for personal use. She had a large cache of the deadly stuff. Nevertheless, in all fairness to Ruby, she was very likely under the influence of the two men. This may have been her first foray into drug sales, and her sentence, were there to be one, could well be humane – just sharp enough to obtain her sincere undertaking to leave off this nefarious business for good.

However, the *Collins* decision is about much more than when Ruby could get back to caring for her kids. It set standards, quite restrictive ones, on when and how peace officers can search and seize. It swung the pendulum far in the direction of personal privacy and far away from relatively fear-free living for the rest of us. In our perilous present moment, values, ethics and morals are changing fast – often not for the better. One person's "Leave me alone" can too easily cover up acts that hurt others. Someone's "You can't search me" can deny, say, a woman's right to walk by herself unafraid after dark – in itself a grave and ubiquitous curtailment of liberties. (The Canadian Centre for Justice Statistics reports that women are four times more likely than men to feel unsafe walking alone at night in their area, and three times more likely to be afraid at home alone after dark.[2])

Another side-effect of the *Collins* ruling, I should add, is that some goal-oriented peace officers often simply ignore it. Say there's been a rash of shoplifting in a mall. Merchants are upset. An officer sees someone walking away with a shopping bag. Something in the person's looks, his walk, twigs the officer's sixth sense and he collars him. There's a slight tremor in the fellow's voice while the officer searches his bag. If he finds stolen goods, he may leave it at that. There's no point in laying charges after such an illegal search. Those stolen goods could have been, at other times, a concealed hand gun or a switch blade knife – even a remote-control device to detonate a car bomb.

Which leads to an irony. With the state our laws are in, upright citizens may now be stopped, questioned – even frisked – on the streets by concerned officers who believe they have grounds to do so. These citizens may pay a price in privacy, inconvenience and annoyance. But guilty citizens reap a benefit. In the case of stolen goods, they have to surrender them but cannot be charged – leaving them to go on with their felonious ways.

Little wonder that the number of criminals prosecuted in Canada is so tiny, compared to the number of crimes committed. Although there is a social, as well as a legal, factor at work here, it is worth noting a national boast of the Danes – "few in Denmark have too much, while fewer have too little." And, they maintain, only two percent of their budget is spent on policing, protection and corrections. Not so in Canada, where we spend incalculably more.

When Privacy is Violated

Of course, safeguards must be put in place to prevent State intrusion into personal space – the space that fosters individual personality. And we can't deny that rights without remedies are meaningless. But there are direct and effective safeguards against unreasonable searches that do not involve disqualifying good evidence.

Foremost is the right to sue for damages in the civil courts when personal privacies have been unduly invaded. An award of damages against law enforcement officials and their employer is the surest way to make them carry on their work in a fair and just manner. In fact, Chapter 9 of the B.C. Privacy Act (1968) allows tort damages to anyone whose privacy is willfully and unreasonably disturbed, depending on the nature and degree of the violation, by either the State or an individual. Under this, an employer could be sued for installing hidden cameras in toilets to curb employee theft, and the enterprising New Zealand private eye who sold the client list from a weight-loss clinic to a chocolate factory could be sued.

All unreasonable trespasses on personal privacies – a wide range – should be actionable with legal aid assistance in appropriate cases. This is the best deterrent and redress. As Justice Zuber wrote (in the Duguay decision already cited), "There is no satisfactory evidence that the exclusion of evidence is effective as a mechanism for control of police methods." To which I add that, when otherwise good evidence is excluded, the penalty is paid by the public, not by the offender.

An aggrieved citizen may also register a complaint under police disciplinary codes. In well-founded and serious cases, this can and should result in hearings, penalties and compensations.

Further, when police or other official misconduct breaches the criminal laws – say assault, perjury or the planting of false evidence – a remedy lies in a prosecution launched by the attorney-general. Such law-breaking, it should be added, is more likely to be encouraged than deterred by needlessly restrictive evidentiary rules. These rules are resented by officers who may be tempted to find ways around them, or to tailor their testimony to make the evidence appear admissible.

Moreover, if in the course of a trial a judge hears that the accused or a witness has been mistreated, he or she can report the matter to the attorney-general or to a police commission. Where the mistreatment truns out to be gross in relation to the gravity of the offence, the judge can "stay" the charges against the accused. It has been the courts' jurisdiction since time immemorial to see that "equity is done." That power may be exercised without putting a judge in the dubious position of having to ignore the truth of what happened.

The "Stay" – A Better Way

The notion of privacy rights was still in its infancy in 1952, when one Jules Rochin made it to the U.S. Supreme Court.[3] Three police officers had followed him home, thinking he was into narcotics. Breaking into his house, they found him in bed, hurriedly swallowing two capsules from his night table. Off they hustled him to a hospital, where aides strapped him down and proceeded to pump his stomach, retrieving the capsules. They were morphine. The U.S. court held that their actions had been "so abusive of individual privacy as to shock the conscience." His charges were stayed – that is, he was sent on his way, without a determination of his guilt.

121

Put Rochin's case side by side with Ruby Collins's – the offences are much alike. When you consider their circumstances, both come down to moral decisions and questions of fact to be decided by judges or juries. In good conscience, Rochin should have been sent home – the brutality really was just too much. But Ruby? Were the methods used extreme? Free societies occasionally must use harsh means to uphold the rules that allow people to live together in peace and security.

Let's have another look at a case where charges were stayed. This one took place in B.C. in 1994, when a Provincial Court judge stayed theft charges against one Brian Wilson.[4] Wilson had shoplifted $52 worth of meat. A private security guard saw him do it, followed him to his car and called on him to stop – but failed to identify himself as a guard. Wilson began to drive off with his purloined tenderloin, his car door open. The guard jumped into the passenger seat and applied a life-threatening carotid hold to Wilson, whose right arm had been amputated some years previously. He lapsed into unconsciousness, but subsequently recovered.

At trial, the judge, in staying the charges, held that the guard's degree of force was disproportionate to the seriousness of the offence. (Licensed guards, by the way, fall under the Charter.) But on appeal, a Supreme Court judge ruled that the stay was not appropriate. Instead, he found enough evidence of theft prior to the assault in the car and convicted Wilson. With all due respect, the lower court's stay was a better and more just response to the guard's abusive behaviour. At the same time, it did *not* eradicate good evidence.

Rochin, as we have seen, was searched in his own home. When can peace officers "reasonably" search a home? It's a fair question, as more criminal doings move indoors. Pot cultivators grow marijuana under 600-volt sodium lights; amphetamines are mixed up in the bath tub. An animal-rights extremist can concoct a home-made bomb using nitrate fertilizer; a gun addict can assemble an illegal arsenal in a closet. Everyday life becomes not only terminal, but downright dangerous.

The Unknowable Law of Vehicle Searches

The automobile is very much part of our dangerous daily life. Our shoplifter friend, Wilson, was seized in his car. As we are about to see,

Anthony Klimchuk had his car searched. What reasonable expectation of privacy should we have while inside our mini-mobile-homes?

Driving around early one morning in a suburb of Victoria, B.C., Klimchuk was fingered by a watchful citizen. There'd been some break-ins of coin-operated machines in the neighbourhood, and this crimestopper had dialled 911 to describe what he thought could be the offender's car. With only this to go on, the patrol officers pulled Klimchuk over and detained him while they searched his car. They found $186 in coins, along with keys that could be used to broach coin-vending devices. He was arrested and escorted to the lock-up.

Had this particular search been "reasonable?" Should the coins and keys be accepted as evidence? As Klimchuk's fortunes wended their way through the courts, there followed as many opinions on these points as there were judges hearing the case.

At Klimchuk's first trial, the judge convicted him, despite some reservations. He considered that: the search was a violation of the rules set out in the Charter's Section 8; the "arbitrary detention" offended Section 9; and the officers had not acted in "good faith" (in its legal sense). Nonetheless, the judge let in the coins and keys as "real evidence," the admissibility of which would not affect "the fairness of the trial."

The Appeal Court, however, acquitted Mr. K.[5] One majority justice held the warrantless search "unreasonable," adding that, in any event, there were insufficient grounds to obtain a warrant or to detain the accused. The same justice stated that there'd been "bad faith" on the part of the legal system, and that admitting the evidence, though "real" enough, would sully the reputation of the Law.

The other majority justice refused to agree on "bad faith" but did find the search to have been illegal. He then decided that, with this "less serious offence," that a fair-minded member of the public would want the evidence excluded as a check on such police misconduct in future. I should add, however, that mercifully, if a similarly inspired search of a car trunk turned up a dead body with gaping wounds, most judges would consider that "real" evidence, and admissible, however illegal or gross the search had been.

The Chief Justice dissented. In his view, "ordinary prudence required some police response." He indicated that there was "urgency," and that the interference with Klimchuk's privacy had been minimal. He further stated that the officers could have "detained" Klimchuk for up to an hour while they got a "tele-warrant" by phone from an all-night justice of the peace. He concluded that, even if the search had been illegal, rejecting the evidence would bring justice into greater disrepute than would admitting it.

Well, here we have a conundrum. Three learned legal eagles, all with widely variant opinions on what some "ordinary, reasonable" citizens would say about this search. Doubtless, Mr. and Ms. Ordinary and Reasonable would take an overall view that balanced individual and general rights. They would grant experienced officers some latitude in the calls they make in stressful encounters. They would have faulted the officers for driving on or taking a coffee break. They'd think "detaining" a motorist for up to an hour while a warrant was sought to be a greater affront to civil liberties than a quick and courteous, but unauthorized, search.

In Britain, with its unwritten constitution, there may be more civility in searches and arrests than in the United States, with its restrictive court-interpreted constitutional "rights." Civil liberties basically rest upon political culture and public attitude. Not to mention that the number of guns is usually in inverse ratio to the amount of civility.

After all, our Charter doesn't constitutionalize detailed rules of conduct. Rules bristle with uncertainties and exceptions, their boundaries shrinking and expanding year by year. No one can foresee the infinite variety of situations that police encounter in their work. To quote Polish poet Wislawa Szymborska, who won the Nobel Prize for Literature in 1996: "Nothing can ever happen twice; No day copies yesterday."

If this is confusing for the average, ordinary, responsible Canadian, imagine how the police feel. As our law now stands, officers cannot predict, except in obvious cases, what the courts will finally say about the choices they have to make. This situation does not make for high job satisfaction, let alone the unhampered pursuit of good order and public safety.

A Manual for Transporting Booty

Three young women, out on a felonious frolic, drove down a busy highway near Cambridge, Ontario. It was 8:30 p.m. on June 5, 1991. They were pulled over for speeding. Ms. Belnavis, at the wheel, said she had borrowed the car from her boyfriend. After making a computer request for information, the officer returned to the car to look for documentation and noticed open garbage bags crowding the back-seat passenger. The bags contained new clothes, with visible price tags, and differing explanations were offered by the car's occupants as to whose bag was whose.

When the computer belched out information about Ms. Belnavis, it turned out she was wanted under an outstanding warrant for unpaid traffic tickets. The officer arrested her, unable to stop himself from thinking he was on to more than random petty theft. Searching the car incident to the arrest, he turned up more tagged new clothing stashed in the trunk. In Ms. Belnavis's purse, he found 12 pairs of brand-new women's panties. He had the car towed, and all three women, one a teen, were charged with possession of stolen goods. However, all were acquitted at trial after evidence of the clothes was excluded. Why? A traffic stop turning into a search for stolen goods? No Charter way!

The Crown appealed. Onward and upward to the Supreme Court,[6] which held that the driver, although not the owner, had "a reasonable expectation of privacy in the vehicle." For her, accordingly, the search was a Charter breach. But the passenger had no such expectation, either as to the car or the goods seized. So no breach for her.

However, the majority held that regardless of whether the search was "reasonable," the trial judge had misdirected himself in excluding the evidence. He had failed to give enough consideration to "society's interests in the effective prosecution of crime," and to the fact that "the evidence was essential to the prosecution and entirely reliable." A new trial was ordered.

In the fullness of time, the case was revived (as Lawyer said to Client in Dickens's *Bleak House,* "the case does not sleep. We wake it up, air it, walk it about..."), and a fresh decision reached. But first, a word from on high to patrol officers: When you arrest for a traffic violation, you may secure your own safety. That said, you run some risk of turning up a more serious offence. Second, to those making off with contraband, allow me to summarize the important points of this case, which should be required reading for aspiring felons:

- Drive (and breathe) normally. Do not speed. Check your turn signals.

- Do not leave stolen goods in plain view. Stow them in the trunk.

- Do not take turns at the wheel. Let the one more seriously involved, who the courts have told us has a higher expectation of privacy, do the driving.

- If questioned, follow standard legal advice: Do not disclose anything more than you must.

- Finally, a word to shopkeepers. It may be costly, but insurance coverage is a necessity these days. You'll get little help from the courts.

Another Close Shave For the Law

In 1993, a Manitoba wildlife warden, James Kamann, observed a car parked by a rural road. In the open field some 10 to 15 metres off the road, he spotted a man who appeared to pop up out of the *veldt*. Could this be a hunting violation? But the man, a Mr. Castlake, claimed he was using the field as a biffy. "I repaired into the tall grasses to relieve myself," he said when challenged. Still, the warden had his doubts. Why was Castlake so fidgety and nervous? So after the man drove off, the warden went to the place where he'd first seen Castlake. There he retrieved a yellow garbage bag containing nine pounds of marijuana.

A Mountie shortly took charge of Mr. Castlake and had the man's car towed to a garage for impoundment. However, this officer was alone – his only partner was away on other duties – and it was not until six hours later that he went to the garage to search the car and do an inventory. (This is standard procedure, to protect the car-owner's valuables and perhaps find other evidence.)

Bingo! A quantity of cocaine was tucked under the driver's seat. The counts were now twofold: trafficking both in soft and in hard drugs. When the latter count went to appeal, the High Court found itself in a real pickle.[7]

What confused the Justices? That the car had been searched for marijuana, but cocaine was found – and not until six hours after the arrest. A warrantless search, so long postponed, was deemed "*prima facie* unreasonable" and not "truly incidental to the arrest." Clearly, in their eyes, a Charter violation. Still, in a near thing, the cocaine was not expunged from judicial memory. Castlake did go down in the High Court, after all, and the Law was not cheated of its prey.

Which leaves us to ponder the question of when a search is "truly incidental" to an arrest? Ah, if only officers could take a judge with them when they go out on patrol. Only one, mind you, not two. Two may well disagree.

Home Sweet Pot Farm

Our rising expectations of privacy are exalted by historical tradition, dating from 1763, when William Pitt the Elder told the British Parliament, "The poorest man in his cottage may bid defiance to all the forces of the Crown. It may be frail, its roof may shake, the rain may enter, but the King cannot enter; all his force dare not cross the threshold of the ruined tenement."

So the question becomes crucial: When can peace officers "reasonably" invade our modern-day citadels? Read on, for yet another opinion.

George Kokesch[8] wasn't all that dangerous. Still, he found that his home was indeed his castle, because he had the law in his corner. Drug officers had, on a tip, tracked him to his house on Vancouver Island, sneaking over his lawn to peer through heavily curtained windows. There, they heard the humming sound of electricity in the air, and through a vent they smelled "a slight odour of marijuana."

That was on Day One, when they obtained enough grounds to get a search warrant. On Day Two, with the warrant in hand, they burst in on Farmer K and seized both him and his crop. However, the Supreme Court held (by a narrow majority) that the illegal trespass that occurred on Day One nullified the warrant search on Day Two. Kokesch was free to carry on, although the experience may have taught him either to watch his electric bills more carefully – they aren't confidential – or to purchase a generator.

In our society, the police must operate under certain restrictive rules. The meter-reader is free to enter to check Kokesch's consumption; the letter carrier can come to the door with an implied licence to trespass (while keeping an eye on the dog); the gas inspector can go inside to check the furnace; and the building inspector can sniff disdainfully at the renovations. But peace officers, with only hunches, have to keep to the sidewalk. They may, on occasion, conduct "knock-on" investigations. But not if they are trying to detect some tell-tale smell when the door opens. Nor can they let a sniffing dog run up to a window; its sniff would be a "search" without prior probable cause.

Again, the Charter stresses that searches must be "reasonable," and how that term is defined depends upon the circumstances in each case. It is futile to lay down legalistic rules in advance as to what may turn out to be reasonable.

What the Camera Could Not See

In a case known as *The Queen v Wong*[9], a hotel room had been converted into an illegal public gambling den. Yet, in the eyes of a majority of the Supreme Court, this room was as much an impenetrable refuge as someone's home.

Of course, most people don't advertise events in their homes by distributing flyers in the streets and restaurants to notify interested gamblers of the times and dates of floating sessions. When you invite all and sundry to come and have a fling with Lady Luck, surely you can't expect the usual rules of privacy to apply.

Yes, indeed you can, said the High Court judges. The players enjoyed the privacy of those who "retire to a hotel room and close the door behind them," they ruled. Only Chief Justice Lamer dissented, pointing out that even undercover cops could have answered the organizers' invitation.

The gamblers had been carefully surveyed by undercover officers who, with the help of the hotel keeper, installed a video camera in the room's drapery valance. (There was no sound component, since third-party sound taps require a special warrant.) On the third night, after reviewing the film, the lawmen swooped in, scooping up promoters, gambling paraphernalia and big sums of cash on the tables. The ring-leaders, duly charged, began their long, slow trek to the Supreme Court.

Before we go on, consider whether their trespasses should have been forgiven. How harmful was this illegal pastime? Wasn't it just a sporting fling, an indulgence no more sinful than buying a ticket on the 6/49? Risky enough, I'd say. Forgetting government's loss of its gaming cut, the real harm caused by gambling is the all-too-common family destitution resulting from gambling addicts betting their last penny against a stacked deck or loaded dice.

In fact, to my mind, just as much harm was done by the judgement – in this case harm to the Law. As well as the Court's strange miscalculation about the privacy of the hotel room, it also threw out reliable evidence recorded by the video camera, while admitting less reliable oral testimony.

The police could have saved themselves the trouble and expense of video surveillance by merely placing an informer in that room, especially since this species is likely to testify to whatever his contractor wishes to hear. Or a sore loser could have been inveigled to take the stand against his "friends." Officers in the next room could even have put their ears to the wall or drilled a peep-hole. Would any of these questionable techniques pro-duced more reliable evidence than the camera?

Proliferating rules as to the reasonableness of unreasonableness easily becomes unreasonable. In *Wong,* they led to absurdity. For one thing, is it real-ly the *place* that gives a high or low expectation of privacy? What if you are in your home, bringing dank deeds to a boil? Or driving on a Los Angeles freeway, with a helicopter clattering overhead? Or in your bank, your every transaction recorded on film – after all, is money not more private then sex in our society? Surely it is the balance that should matter – public security on one side of the scale, and the degree of intrusion on the other.

In Britain today, police officers are empowered to pick up truants, whose ranks have been swelling, and take them to school. Courts are now able to make parenting orders and levy fines against mothers and fathers who per-sistently fail to send their kids to class. A decision has been made to sacrifice privacy in favour of preventing the social fall-out of uneducated youngsters, on the loose and unsupervised, getting into all kinds of trouble.

Denmark, hard-hit by Hell's Angels, has banned their clubs and motorcy-cle gangs. Police can search and detain them on sight, civil liberties be damned.

And where was my expectation of privacy recently at the Vancouver International Airport? Infringed by a drug-sniffing dog. A customs officer escorted me to a special room and meticulously searched my bags. "My pro-file," I told her, "has at long last given me away." "No," she replied, "our dog was just 'interested' in you."

When Detectives Work to Rule

Josh Borden's right to bodily privacy enabled him to get his rape con-viction lifted.[10] In December of 1989, Borden was arrested for sexually assaulting an exotic dancer in the Sundowner Motel in Montreal. She iden-tified him in a photo line-up. But the detectives on the case suspected that Josh was also the perpetrator of the brutal rape of an elderly women two months earlier. That victim could not identify her assailant, as he had covered her face with her comforter. Still, he had left semen stains on that comforter.

Naturally, police wanted a sample of Borden's blood for a DNA test. This they could not obtain without his consent. So they led him to think they wanted the sample on connection with the assault on the exotic dancer.

Borden okayed this, sure he had left behind no bodily fluids on that occasion.

The DNA test did connect Borden with the brutal rape. He appealed as far as the Supreme Court, arguing that he had been beguiled by the police into giving his consent. That court agreed and upset his conviction.

Now, bearing in mind that officers have an on-going duty to solve any crimes that come their way, I suggest that the detectives' subterfuge in obtaining Borden's blood was reasonable. Carefully used, deception is an accepted part of police work – consider the undercover officer and the paid police informer, not to mention the infiltrator of a neo-Nazi gang. If Borden's fingerprint, legally taken on his arrest, had tied him to the earlier rape, his conviction would have stood.

The *Borden* decision, amid a storm of public criticism, lit a fire under the federal government, and Parliament quickly provided that blood samples could be taken without consent when a judge "is satisfied there are reasonable grounds to believe that a suspect is guilty of a sexual or violent offence." (This Criminal Code amendment was passed in 1995.) Those "reasonable grounds" – a fertile field indeed – will doubtless be contested in many courts, high and low. In Borden's case, they were held not to exist. But the point missed is that giving something as simple as a blood sample to help clear up a crime is surely part of the dues anyone owes as a citizen.

Parliament Legitimizes "Reprehensible Police Behaviour"

Prior to application of that Code amendment, Justice Peter Cory, for the Supreme Court majority, had this to say: [11]

"Bodily samples could not be taken incident to an arrest, as a search so invasive in an 'affront to human dignity.'"

He was referring to the trial for the murder of 14-year-old Pamela Bischoff, who had been with a group of seven teenagers, six years earlier, on April 12, 1991, partying in the woods in New Brunswick's Oromocto region. After drinking beer and wine, and sharing some LSD, one of the teens, 17-year-old Billy Stillman, left the group with Pamela. Stillman arrived at his home at midnight, cold, shaken and wet. He had a cut above one eye and mud and grass on his pants. He said he had been in a fight with five Indians.

Pamela's body was found six days later, near a bridge over a nearby river.

An expert placed the time of her death at around 11 p.m. on April 12. She had not drowned; her death was caused by wounds to the head. Semen was found in her vagina, and she had a human bite-mark on her abdomen. A motorist had seen her by the bridge with a young man about 10 p.m. Another witness saw Stillman walking from the bridge close to midnight.

Stillman was arrested and, over time, gave differing explanations for his condition and where he had last seen Pamela. His lawyer, well-versed, then gave the police a letter, saying his client had been advised to say nothing and not to consent to the taking of any body-fluid samples. Nevertheless, the police used force to take some hair, pubic included. A buccal swab and a Plasticine impression of his teeth were also obtained. Stillman sobbed but refused to answer questions. He went to the washroom, blew his nose on a tissue and threw it into a waste bin, and this was also collected as evidence. The hair, swab, Plasticine impression and tissue were all sent for DNA and other tests. Meanwhile, without enough evidence to detain him, police had to release Stillman.

Several months later, after the test results came in, he was re-arrested. A dentist took another impression of his bite. Transferred to adult court, he was tried and convicted of first-degree murder.

In the Supreme Court, all Stillman's body samples were held to have been "conscripted," and the judges pronounced "a very serious Charter violation" as "the ultimate invasion of the accused's privacy." Taking samples from Stillman was "a reprehensible and flagrant" disregard of his rights. Even collecting the used tissue was adjudged to be a constitutional violation. Every scrap of evidence, except for the tissue he'd blown his nose on and "abandoned," was suppressed. Not to reject it would, the judges averred, "shock fair-minded members of the community." But in the case of parents all over Canada, it was the rejection of the evidence that was so shocking.

A re-trial was ordered, with only Justices Beverley McLachlin and Claire L'Heureux-Dubé, in the minority, affirming Stillman's conviction.

One of the dissenting judges in *Stillman* considered the State's seizure of his samples a "minimal affront to his bodily integrity." Indeed, they were less taxing than most visits to a dentist. And if Stillman was "pressured" to give them, so were men in Vermilion, Alberta, in 1995, when 100 of them anonymously volunteered their blood in a serial-rapist investigation. Not to volunteer, or to leave town for spurious reasons, would have tended to incriminate.

After a similar crime in a small town in Wales, 2,000 men lined up to give DNA profiles, as a matter of civic pride. They were simply doing their duty.

To exempt someone from paying dues, simply because he or she may be guilty, flies in the face of common sense. Likewise, there should be no exemption from taking a road-side breath test, even if you're as sober as a judge. What is considered "reasonable" depends on many factors, including the damage caused by the crime. For instance:

- You don't have to open your door to a uniformed officers on a house-to-house "dragnet" investigation after a murder. But is it not "reasonable" for the officer to knock and to say, authoritatively, "I would like to ask you some questions"?

- Would it be unreasonable for police officers to plant a quarter-sized bug in the sofa of a hotel room to pick up the chitchat of consenting adults engaged in legal gambling? (A stubborn jury, thinking that worse things go on legally in casinos and hotels, might find a way to let the prey escape. Later, a civil jury might award damages for intrusive invasion of privacy.)

- Is it reasonable to demand random urine tests for athletes?

- Should government be permitted to look through border travel declarations to see if some cheaters are holidaying at the expense of unemployment insurance? Should the Privacy Commission hold this to be an "unreasonable" invasion of privacy?

And what about these situations?

- Should the Charter rights of students who carry knives or drugs into school protect them from frisks ordered by the principal? Or from random searches of lockers?

- Faced with multi-million-dollar organized tobacco smuggling in Ontario and Quebec, is it "reasonable" to slash taxes, thus making cigarettes more easily available to teens? Or should officers assigned to stop the trafficking have broader powers to search truck-loads, the truck drivers and mailed packages?

With serious crime, our expectations of privacy, at home or on the streets, must give way, albeit rarely, to social exigencies — and these can be very demanding. When a serial killer is on the loose, police may randomly knock on many doors, asking for leads, sniffing out clues. When they arrived at Paul Bernardo's door, so many years back, he answered but easily averted suspicion with his sociopathic pleasantries. Had that officer had the authority to search Bernardo's home, he might have seen straps, or bruises on Karla Homulka's face, or something else that hinted at the goings-on in the household. And another young life might have been saved.

Personal Privacy and Public Security Must Get Along

In a perfect world, we would all be free to seek self-fulfillment in our own ways. Robinson Crusoe, alone on his tropical island, could do that – at least until the tide washed up the redoubtable Friday. After that, Crusoe was living in a community. All the castaway's do-my-own-thing activities were now subject to respect for another, and the pair had to work out some give-and-take.

Today, in our crowded cities, where many are up to no good, we have far more privacy than did our forefathers in medieval villages, where everyone knew everything about everybody. Today, our law enforcement is unduly hampered, what with assaults on abortion clinics, excessive tolerance of firearms in private hands and computer fraud growing ever more profitable than drug-running or tax evasion. Sophisticated conspirators charge illegal immigrants $50,000 each to be smuggled into Canada. Court decisions are not wisely fostering "the safety and the health of the whole state." [12] They are not keeping up with the times. Back in 1910, the famous English constitutional authority, A.V. Dicey, told a lecture audience that "judge-made law occasionally represents the opinion of the day before yesterday." That's just not good enough anymore: it must represent the needs of the day after tomorrow.

Pop Quiz

You're getting the hang of it now, Dear Reader. Contrarity rules; common sense languishes. Test your credulity on the following two cases:

1. A young man, cell phone in his ear, knocks on a friend's door. He is shown in, to his horror, by three narcs who are executing a drug warrant.

"Empty your pockets," they demand. The young man does so, and reveals possession of crack cocaine. He has a luckier day when he comes to court. His judge thinks the narcs should discover evidence, not let it stumble on them. He rules there was no "articulable" cause to search the young man. Case dismissed.[13]

Question: Kindly articulate the judgement you would have pronounced, had you been sitting on the bench that day.

2. A young man leaves his footprints at a murder scene. He is taken into custody, and officers demand a set of his footprints. He objects, but consents when they tell him, "We'll take them anyway." The footprints match those at the scene.

At trial, the judges rule that the forcible taking of footprints is not like a forced confession, and allow the footprints to do the talking. The fellow is convicted.[14]

Question: Do you agree with the judges, or do you think the young man should having told police (quoting Groucho), "If you want my footprints, go get them yourself. They're upstairs in my socks."?

Chapter 8

Picking Pockets with a Rake-Off

"Laws are like cobwebs, which may catch small flies,
but let wasps and hornets break through."
— Jonathan Swift, *"A Critical Essay"*

Compared with the multi-millions of dollars pocketed in financial frauds, the spoils of crimes committed with a jimmy, a gun or a knife are paltry. Yet Canadians no longer believe that our legal system is capable of bringing the perpetrators of serious frauds to justice. And they are quite right. Clever and determined swindlers all too often outwit and outrun our cumbersome and rusty law-enforcement procedures.

Commercial and financial frauds come in all sizes and shapes, from the darkly criminal to the commonplace conflict of interest. Frauds are simply lies told to someone to get hands on their stuff. Conflicts of interest are the misuse of office for personal gain. Commercial crimes run the gamut from salting ore samples to bilking credulous investors to influence-peddling by politicians on the take. They include dastardly deeds such as cooking the books to hike stock prices, trading in confidential information, walking away leaving suppliers holding the bag, inflating bills for services rendered, milking the public purse by evading taxes (not just avoiding them – the difference is six months!)

and rigging bids. Fund managers use their position to buy shares on the sly; purchasers collect kickbacks from suppliers; credit-card scammers cheat retailers; hackers break into corporate or government computers – whatever the swindle, there's always an itchy palm in the picture, and never an itchy conscience.

Generally, these misdeeds are veiled from public view, although we do enjoy occasional glimpses of inexplicable riches, luxury automobiles and exotic vacations in the watering-holes of the wealthy.

The perpetrators, for the most part, wear white collars and three-piece suits and enjoy six-figure incomes. They are persons of high social status and influence. Ordinary blue- and pink-collar types can't fiddle their tax returns to any lucrative extent and have little use for offshore banks. Their crimes are pettier – shoplifting, B&Es, the odd hold-up. But the big boys (and a small but creative number of big girls) have crunched the numbers and realize that it's more efficient to bilk a million people of a dollar each than to hold up 100 banks for an average take of $10,000.

Financial swindles are by no means victimless crimes. The wounds of those hapless folk foolish enough to trust a charlatan can smart as much as those of someone mugged on the street. A friendly house call by a huckster peddling a "safe" investment, his false pretenses hidden beneath smiles and assurances, can cost an old couple their life savings and leave them with a bitter feeling that they were partly to blame for being so gullible. What price their loss of trust in social institutions, their shattered dreams, their compromised health?

Still, Canada's courts seem reluctant to treat white collar crime and white collar criminals as harshly as they do those at the other end of the social spectrum. Consider the fate of Senator Michel Cogger. The punishment meted out for his proven conflict of interest could hardly be considered cruel and unusual. Cogger was convicted of pocketing $212,000 while in office for aiding a businessman trying to land a $45 million government grant. His sentence? No prison time, a $3,000 fine and 240 hours of community service. Nor did his sins cost him his seat in the Senate.

You have to wonder what elitist flight of fancy led the Supreme Court in 1991 to say that business frauds were not "true crimes."[1] That's a dubious moral position! A breach of business regulations can be as true a crime as cheating the welfare system. Indeed, the bite may be deeper, and the teeth sharper. In truth, the depth of criminality depends on the amount of harm the offence inflicts on victims and society. It should be judged by the conduct of the offender, and certainly not on the colour of the collar he or she wears.

In the case which spurred this dubious utterances by the High Court, concerning false advertising by a travel agency named Wholesale Travel, the Chief Justice spoke of "true" and "untrue" crimes. He had this to say of business illegalities:

> "...the stigma associated with these offences is not analogous to the stigma of dishonesty which would attach to a conviction for theft."

He obviously viewed false advertising as small potatoes. But such misdeeds can drive an honest competitor into bankruptcy and rob a customer. Human misery is the real cost of fraud, along with a decoupling of merit and reward that erodes the moral fibre of society and makes honesty a losing proposition.

Wholesale Travel was just one case in which the courts have set stumbling blocks in the path of expeditious and effective fraud-prevention and prosecution. Sharp or shady dealing has as long a pedigree as any other human failing, dating back even before the time when some con artist gulled a naive lad named Jack out of the family cow in exchange for a handful of beans. Felicitous law-keeping does, occasionally, overcome these hurdles. For instance, back on March 3, 1795, this entry appeared in the *Kentish Gazette* in southeastern England:

> "The Mayor of Canterbury and some Justices of the Peace visited the butter market. They found the butter of two persons considerably deficient in weight. They ordered the same to be taken and delivered to the Sheriff for the use of the poor prisoners in the west-gate gaol. And they admonished them not to offend again in like manner."

The good mayor and his fellows had made a quick appraisal of the situation and administered humane correction. They knew that when one person strays from honest dealing, others will follow suit — if only to preserve their own profits and place. In the interests of preserving their own local tax base, they also knew that customers could desert to other marketplaces after suffering a loss of confidence and trust, not to mention of shillings and pence.

Some 40 years later, also in Kent, a baker did not get off so lightly. He was caught slipping bits of iron into the loaves he sold by weight. He was whipped, fined and sentenced to a stretch in prison. The magistrates of the day were clearly of the view that his was a "true" crime.

Alas, in our enlightened times, the penalties appear to have softened. In 1996, in Vancouver, two shysters ran up the shares of their metal-refining company by slipping bars of brass into their gold inventory. Caught in the act, their fines were probably not as high as their legal bills, and their company was only temporarily suspended from the local stock exchange. The law did work, at least to some extent, but such wrist-slapping is unlikely to prevent recidivism.

But when it comes to really grandiose manipulation of the financial markets, the law falters. Jonathan Swift really knew what he was talking about.

A Scam Made in Canada

The financial shenanigans of the Alberta mining company, Bre-X, were far from decently veiled. They unfolded with front-page headlines, smack in the public eye. Following the company's announcement of the "biggest-ever" find of gold in Indonesia, its share values ratcheted up to $280 from pennies, and the company was suddenly worth billions. Not bad for an outfit that never sold an ounce of gold and never turned a profit. Here was a hold-up that left the Law in the dust, unable to get a handle on what was really going on, either before or after the collapse.

The Bre-X promoters, visible and invisible, followed a script that should have been familiar to anyone knowledgeable about Canadian mining circles. After all, this was our third case of mega gold mine salting in recent memory. Each left, at the denouement, one dead body with a loose tongue.

Bre-X played out in typical fashion. First, in 1995, there was the "find." Then, the stream of feel-good press releases, sales pitches, soaring stock prices that enticed even mutual funds. Then, a year later, the quiet unloading of stock gains in millions by those in the know; the proposed sale to a big mining conglomerate; tests showing the drill samples had been coated with placer gold (not even drilled gold!) en route to the assay lab; and the final collapse.

On the upswing, hundreds of lucky punters sold out in time with six figure capital gains to declare. On the plunge, thousands had their margins called and lost fortunes. Two committed suicide.

With the horse out of the barn and galloping over the hills, the Law slowly swung into action. There was an RCMP investigation and civil suits against Bre-X, once more a shell, and against brokerage firms for negligence. Defence lawyers insisted that fraud and conspiracy could not be proved. Some well-covered tracks were uncovered, and detailed books written.

A well-crafted scheme and no more honest than a bank hold-up, Bre-X should have been nipped in the bud, but wasn't. Once more, in the commercial crime marketplace, justice was sold short.

Confronted with misdoings in trade and commerce, Canadians have three options. First, we can lay charges in our criminal courts, inevitably running the gauntlet of Charter objections. Second, we can encourage victims to sue in the civil courts, if they can afford the costs and have a fair likelihood of being able to collect on a judgement. Third, we can set up specialized agencies, endowed with the power to inspect, forestall, detect, redress and punish.

You might think our courts would go out of their way to help such specialized agencies do their work. They have a tough enough time carrying out their mandates. Instead, with the birth of the Charter, these agencies – mercifully they do exist – have encountered one impediment after another.

The Public Will Never Know

In 1980, Canada's two largest newspaper chains, Southam and Thomson, were joined together in matrimony. Canadians suddenly found that their English dailies, in Montreal, Vancouver, Winnipeg and Ottawa, had but one parent. People protested, worried the merging fever could be infectious, as it would prove to be. Parliament ordained a Royal Commission, and its combines agency began to look into restraint of trade practice – one company nationwide in control of the price of newspaper ads! Of circulation! Of ultimate news selection! Charges were laid and an "order" was proclaimed in 1982, under statutory authority, allowing investigators to check documents that might point to collusion or to undue restriction of competition. Search warrants followed.

All in vain. For the courts were to have their nay-say. Never mind that they were dealing with an event of momentous social and economic significance. They quashed the search order even before any searching had taken place. What might have been turned up, the public will never know.

The Supreme Court set its seal of approval on this denial of the public right to know in 1984, in a case known as *Hunter v Thomson*.[2] The lasting harm is in the precedents the Court laid down in coming to its decision. These made it harder for specialized agencies to prevent, let alone prosecute, unlawful business practices.

First, it took the word "everyone" in a Charter legal-rights section and misinterpreted it. The section reads: "Everyone has a right to be secure against unreasonable search or seizure." The Court said "everyone" included companies – far from what those who sired the Charter intended. The sires (all men, incidentally; Canadian women need feel no collective culpable guilt over its conception) sold the Charter as the safeguarding of individual rights and liberties. They purposefully excluded the protection of property rights. Companies, of course, only exist to hold property. In the simplest way of looking at it, they themselves are property. Besides, wherever else the word "everyone" is used in the Charter, it applies only to individuals.

Moreover, in an earlier decision the Court had ruled that companies did not fall within the term "everyone." In *Hunter v Thomson,* it reversed this decision, and in doing so added a weapon to the arsenals of companies resisting public monitoring by agencies set up to do just that.

Second, the Court held that agencies could not inspect company records without first establishing on oath, "credibility based on probability, replacing suspicion," that an offence had taken place. This puts a stop to inspections conducted as a preventive measure against a likely or possible offence taking place. And, where an offence had taken place, the public pretty well has to prove it has occurred before being able to see the important evidence.

Third, the Court, philosophically, based its decision on a company's "expectation of privacy" with respect to its business records. That gives companies more protection against appropriate public inspection than citizens have. Suppose you are asked by an officer to produce your driver's licence, car registration and proof of insurance. You do it, because there is a compelling public interest. Or suppose you enlarge your living room. A zoning inspector can enter your home and measure the area. But suppose a major company may be into price-fixing at the expense of many thousands of citizens. Isn't there an equal, or greater, compelling interest in public examination of its business documents? The Supreme Court of Canada says no.

Is it possible to conclude from this that something is seriously amiss with our laws? If you are in any doubt, the long-winded Doman-Bennett case should change your mind. If all were well with the Law, how could the resolution of a simple point take so long and cost so much? How could a judge of the criminal court fail to grasp the truth when it was within easy reach? And how could defence lawyers turn a securities commission hearing into a steeplechase that also became a marathon?

Calling a Man About a Horse

At precisely 10:09 a.m. on November 4, 1988, the phone rang in the offices of the Bennett brothers in Kelowna, B.C. Both men were there – Bill, a former B.C. premier, and R.J., a horse fancier. On the line was their old pal Herb Doman, calling from his lumber company headquarters in Duncan, a small town on Vancouver Island. Doman wanted to explain to R.J. why a cheque he'd sent to pay for a horse they had trained had read $500 and not $5,000.[3] "Champers," after cracking its sesamoid, had left racing to become a saddle horse. The poor nag would not survive to see the end of the legal proceedings that were to result from this phone call.

Indeed, was this call just about a horse? Or was it, as B.C. and Ontario securities cops suspected, an illegal tip on the stock market? That's the kind of question courts and securities commissions are supposed to answer. But eight years and trillions of words later, the real reason for Doman's call remained shrouded in legal fog.

Eight years! Yes, the technicalities that have infested criminal law are gumming up the proceedings of securities commissions and other regulatory bodies. Set up to police harmful business practices, to protect people from being cheated in various ways, such organizations – if allowed to do their work fairly and quickly – can nip scams in the bud. But hobbled by nit-picking and lawyerly quibbles, as they are today, these regulatory bodies are hard-pressed to do their jobs.

In the Bennett affair, the circumstances were simple enough. From documents and the timing of the phone calls (not their content; they weren't earwigged), we've learned a few facts.[4]

During the spring and summer of 1988, a growing Oregon lumber giant, Louisiana-Pacific, was quietly buying shares in Doman's company (with Herb Doman's approval). During this period, many Doman-Bennett calls were clocked. At the same time, the Bennett brothers also began to buy Doman shares. By June 1988, Bill Bennett alone had picked up $2.3 million worth of "A" shares at around $7 a pop. Doman's friends and relatives were also buying them, plus some masked purchasers using Swiss banks.

Events unfolded as follows:

- August 1988: Actual take-over negotiations begin. Enter the lawyers, accountants, appraisers et al.

- September and October 1988: The public hear of the affair. One press release discloses the "intended" take-over price for "A" shares as $12. Prices rise accordingly.

- November 4, 1988: Louisiana-Pacific directors breakfast together and decide to call the whole thing off. That morning, between 10:02 and 10:07, their CEO phones Herb Doman to give him the news. He urges Doman to alert the stock exchanges at once to order a "halt trading."

- November 4, 1988: Doman places a five-minute call to Kelowna at 10:09 a.m, about a horse, he later says.

- November 4, 1988: Between 10:14 and 11:11 a.m., the Bennett boys sell off all their 518,000 Doman shares. R.J. even sells others "short." The "A" shares fetch an average of $11.38.

- November 4, 1988: At 11:19 a.m. Doman alerts the Vancouver and Toronto stock exchanges. An immediate "halt trading" ensues.

- November 7, 1988: Trading of Doman shares resumes. The price of "A" shares has dropped to $7.75. Herb Doman is later reported as "devastated"[5] by the turn of events (newspaper articles estimated his loss at $65 million).

Concerned about this scenario, the B.C. and Ontario securities commissions investigated and decided to proceed against the Bennett brothers and Doman. (Other suspects had left no tracks worth pursuing.[6]) They laid charges of insider tipping against the three, with the B.C. charges sidelining the Ontario ones. Judge Wallace Craig of the B.C. Provincial Court presided over a 12-day trial. Presented with the facts as related above, and more (but no evidence from the accused) he dismissed all charges, saying:

"There is no direct evidence [as to] who made the call from Doman's to the Bennett offices or who received the call. It would be speculation at best and cynicism at least to infer that Doman made the call. And to give a sinister connotation to such speculation would lead to a conviction based on suspicion."[7]

Judge Craig not only dismissed criminal charges, he also gratuitously added that, in his opinion, the Crown had not even met a civil standard of proof.

This was what some lawyers term a "finding of fact." The Crown did not appeal. However, the truth of who called whom was well known by the defendants, who were seated within a few feet of the Learned Judge. But, prohibited by our misplaced respect for the accused's right to silence, neither judge nor prosecutor could ask them about it. And for the judge to have weighed in the scales of justice any inference from the defendants' silence would also have been legal sacrilege. Only later, much later, forced to speak up under oath to the Securities Commission, did Doman and the Bennett boys have the horse sense to admit Doman had indeed called R.J.

The acquittal was a stroke of misfortune – for the accused! Had the judge convicted them the first time around, in all likelihood Doman and the Bennett brothers would have made belated amends and cut their losses before the next phase of this legal battle. Because the Securities cops were not about to give up. They pressed on with Commission proceedings.

The defendants' lawyers erected one blocking tactic after another, bouncing the Commission into courts both low and high, "invoking the aid of the Charter." Of course they argued for the protection of our old friend Silence. However, in 1995 the Supreme Court ruled that defendants at commission hearings must talk.[8]

The defence also raised two improbable counts of "bias," one against the commission set-up and one against its members. They raised "issue *estoppel*" – hadn't Judge Craig said there'd been no crime? – and "abuse of power." Next came "multiplicity of proceedings" (the defence lawyers not counting their multiple appeals in that). "Undue delay" by the prosecutors was another objection, a surprising one, given the extent to which the defendants themselves strove to fend off any decision. They also pleaded the Charter's "right to life, liberty and security of person."

But it was all, finally, in vain. On August 28, 1996, the Commission publicly castigated Doman and the Bennett brothers for engaging in "deceit, greed and conspiracy." Their trading privileges were suspended and they were ordered to pay the Commission's hearing costs.

Those were expensive years for the defendants and their reputations. Not only were their misdeeds constantly spotlighted in the media, but they were also sued by one of the big losers in the case, the CBC Pension Fund. This they settled by buying up the Fund's Doman shares at top price, paying $50,000 in damages and $60,000 in legal costs. (The settlement included a hush-hush clause, with a $50,000 penalty if the Fund leaked out the details.)[9]

As for the defendants' legal costs, Bill Bennett – according to the word on the street – spent $2 million trying to hold on to the $2 million he would have made on his Doman shares.

If the Doman–Bennett case taught Canadians anything, it ought to have been this: Don't allow Charter fever to infect the proceedings of regulatory agencies. Such bodies aren't primarily concerned with convictions and punishment; their main purposes are to ensure fair play in the marketplace and to provide environmental safety and protection. Without effective and expeditious enforcement of these regulations, people will buy diseased meat, fly in defective planes, get hit by brakeless trucks, suffer toxic-waste dumping in their neighbourhoods and pay unnecessarily high dispensing fees for lifesaving pharmaceuticals.

Of course, if regulatory tribunals go beyond the powers entrusted to them or deny natural justice to their target, the courts can and should upset their decisions. This is tried-and-true common law. But apart from such limited appeals, the tribunals should be allowed and encouraged to do their jobs, find the facts and make rulings – with far less formality than in the criminal courts.

But when well-off and well-connected malefactors pile up time and expense, regulatory enforcement is ineffective. Any attorney-general with concern for the public purse will call off his dogs. And that could have dire results. Million-dollar commercial scams could multiply, along with more breaches of trust and abuses of office for personal gain. Cheating will proliferate without Justice's vigilance. The loser will be the economy, which suffers when investors' faith is shaken by unscrupulous wheeler-dealers who play confidence games on the stock exchanges.

A prime example of these dire results came to light when Canada's fifth largest insurance company went bankrupt. Confederation Life officials had been lending their policy-holders' money in sweetheart deals to condo and health companies in which they had hidden financial stakes. One of these officials walked away from the financial wreck a much richer man. With a Confederation loan of $2.7 million, he bought shares in the health company that Confederation was keeping in good health and later sold them for a tidy $9 million in capital gains.

Not long ago, such breaches of loyalty to shareholders and clients were quite rare and were prosecuted vigorously. Now the regulators often merely report what they can find out and leave it at that.

A Slippery Slope

We are seeing a slow but steady increase in business immorality, and an uptake in fraud and misdeeds verging on fraud. Here follows a rogues' gallery of sharp practices, all too typical:

- A real estate investment trust raises multi-millions for the purchase of apartment properties. The promoters "co-mingle" investment funds in projects in which they have personal stakes, unjustly enriching themselves at the expense of the investors. But insolvency overtakes the trust and investors lose big. A litigious chase follows, but after five years, hopes grow pale. How many losers were erstwhile friends of the defrauders? Usually it's "Do your friends first; they're easiest."

- The wife of a celebrated English novelist and political mover is an officer in a company. She confides to hubby that good news is about to break. He buys into it and their retirement nest egg is enlarged.

- The chair of a major Canadian shopping-mall corporation negotiates the sale of most of its real estate to a Chicago company, then awards himself a $12 million "commission" for pulling off the sale. It seems not to have occurred to him that he had a trust obligation to serve the best interests of his shareholders in return for his regular remuneration.

Referring to this state of affairs, a hold-up artist recently aired his complaints about corporate corruption. There were three differences, he said, between his small-potatoes ski-mask jobs and big-time financial fraud. First, the little guy was more likely to be caught. Second, fraud spoils made his take look like peanuts. And finally, he didn't harm nearly as many people. He even seemed to harbour a suspicion that the rich get richer and the poor get prison.

Call this fellow cynical, but he does have a point, especially when you examine the courts' record in running down tax evaders who cheat not only the government but all of us who pay our fair share.

An Inspector Calls

In the early 1990s, a Revenue Canada officer, in the course of his employment, began to audit the books of Xentec Lab Inc. and its proprietors. Soon, the inspector formed the opinion that tax offences may have taken place. He was therefore obliged, as a law-abiding public servant, to stop right there and apply for a judicial search warrant. He got his warrant, but his interrupted labours were never to resume. The warrant was challenged in the courts by the company. Why would they do that if they had nothing to hide? Four years later, the matter was quashed by the Supreme Court.

The court's decision affirmed that once a tax inspector "forms the opinion" that his subject may have committed an offence, the Charter kicks in. But this creates an invidious double standard. While the honest taxpayer, with minimal protection, submits to a thorough audit, the dishonest taxpayer uses Charter protection to attack the search warrant, making a federal case of its granting.

When searches are delayed, good public administration is at risk. As one judge pointed out, "There is the attendant risk that if there were any incriminating documents, they might well be concealed in the meantime." [10]

The search warrant in the Xentec case, incidentally, did not go down because the affidavit supporting it lacked "sworn, strong evidence." In fact, it disclosed a specific offence, with incriminating documents to be found in a specific place. The relevant section of the Tax Act says that the judge "shall issue the warrant if satisfied." The courts interpreted this as reducing the judge to a mere "rubber stamp." Others may be forgiven for thinking the judge did have a duty promptly to issue the warrant once he had found "probable cause."

The Supreme Court has nixed what it calls "fishing expeditions"– that is, random spot checks by public officials for the purpose of detecting breaches of law where "true crime" is suspected. The courts often say that the Charter should be given a "generous interpretation." But let it not be generous only for the predator, and niggardly for those preyed upon. The Charter words, "Everyone has a right..." also apply to Mr. and Ms. Average.

No Fishing Allowed

Bait your hook and drop your line. You may catch something. But why shouldn't inspectors have a duty to catch what illegalities they can, in fairness to the public and to business competitors who play fair and square? Some judges have thought that such expeditions would be even more appropriate when tax evasion was actually afoot. Cavanagh, J., in a 1982 case, went on to say that "if the search goes ahead, and nothing incriminating is found, documents are returned, with a possible suit for invasion of privacy, but one which a found defaulter would not win." He was completely overruled. [11]

The Supreme Court rests its case against investigations proceeding where illegalities may be afoot on dubious moral grounds. In the Amway case (*R v Amway Corp.,* [1989] 1 SCR 2), the company was charged with fraudulently marking down the prices of its goods imported into Canada to evade some millions in customs duties. The Court decided that searching of commercial documents can be "an affront to the dignity and privacy of individuals, by their being forced to supply evidence out of their own mouths."

But privacy should not shield business records from officials charged with the responsibility of upholding lawful regulations. Nor, as we have seen, is the doctrine of privacy fairly applied. A butcher can't claim privacy when a health inspector smells and pokes his sausages or calls for receipts to see when and whence they were purchased. Nor can an Olympic weightlifter protest his dignity when a random urine test for steroids is required.

With a well-fixed company, however, inspectors can't even fish for falsely labelled coffee beans. In the late 1980s, one Michael Norton was discovered re-bagging Panamanian coffee beans and selling them to buyers (including Starbucks) as genuine Hawaiian Kona for five times the price. The investigators had to resort to an extensive (and expensive) undercover operation in the U.S., Canada and Europe. Secret informers were deployed, as were telephone taps and surreptitious videos. After legal proceedings finally got underway, Norton was obliged to cough up $1.1 million from a Swiss bank account. This operation did far more harm to civil liberties than allowing an inspector to walk into Norton's place of employment, ask some questions, check invoices and generally sniff around. Norton, by the way, was nailed, despite his defence that "coffee addicts can't tell the difference." [12]

A Positive Duty

Persons and companies choosing to enter into a regulated business have accepted a positive duty to keep records for appropriate inspections, at reasonable times and places. The Lord Chancellor of Britain, Lord Denning, said this of an inspection:

> "If there are circumstances which appear to suggest fraud, misfeasance or other misconduct, the Court should not encourage or support any attempt to delay or hold up the inquiry. The public interest demands it." [13]

Nor should Charter legal rights be allowed to encumber regulatory proceedings, such as in Doman-Bennett. There is no good reason to apply these rights to such proceedings. The defendants were not "persons charged with an offence," as cited in Chapter 5, Section 11. The Charter rights should be confined to the criminal court. The Bennett brothers and Doman chose to play the market. They should be deemed therefore to have agreed to divulge and explain, and to abide by the umpire's decision made in good faith.

Britain's Parliament is moving toward a no-nonsense attack on serious frauds. Section 2 of its 1987 Criminal Justice Act authorizes competent investigators to "obtain information, both written and oral, from individuals or organizations who will not provide it voluntarily." It's about time our Canadian Parliament burst its Charter bonds. It has the power to override decisions that extend special rights to some, with too little respect for the public interest. It need only invoke the "notwithstanding" clause, Section 33 of the Charter. Will it continue to be too cowed by the conventional legal establishment to do so?

When the Law gives generous treatment to predators using sharp practices while offering stingy protection to those preyed upon, more lambs are fleeced, society's values are corrupted and business trust is undermined.

The Quiz

Don't worry – this quick quiz won't snap any attention spans. Simply consider all three of the following white-collar doings, and follow the instructions below.

- Doubting Thomas tax inspectors want a look through a company's books and papers. They know and swear that this company had claimed "false and deceptive" deductions in the previous year, and they obtain a judge's warrant. But the Court of Appeal holds that the judge who issued the warrant had no "standards" in the Act to go on, nor did the warrant specify where to look and what to look for. The case is quashed.[14]

- Agriculture inspectors descend on a tree-and-shrub importer and find gypsy moth infestations in a shipment from three U.S. nurseries. On the spot, judgement is delivered. All the plants are confiscated. The court later ruled that "this businessman had no expectation of privacy from inspectors" and "their emergency action was in order."[15]

- A horse owner at the track in his silver-grey half-ton truck is suddenly set upon by three sleuths employed by the Racing Commission. A scuffle ensues and the sleuths find a hypodermic syringe and various fluid-filled bottles with rubber stoppers. The court eventually rules that "this tout – on the track grounds – had given 'implied consent' to have happen what did happen."[16]

Kindly grade the above activities in order of their potential to inflict harm on society and their relative moral blameworthiness. Then say which gets the most Teflon protection from law enforcement. A short answer should suffice, but if you are not sure of the sense of what you are writing, you may (like a Supreme Court justice) go as long as 60 pages.

Chapter 9

Sunlight Is the Most Powerful of Disinfectants[1]

"No light, but rather darkness visible."

– John Milton, *Paradise Lost*

W ell, canny Reader, you have played your cards well. You are now Her Majesty's attorney-general of Ontario. But it's not just another day at the office. You are taking a lot of heat from the voters, who want you to eradicate the spreading cigarette-smuggling business. They know – and you know – that crates of contraband cigs are pouring through the permeable southern border of your province, and that networks distribute them coast to coast.

There is big money to be made, thanks to a chasm between the untaxed cost of a packet of smokes and the retail price. Regular law enforcement is failing to make much of a dent in this trade. Governments have cried "Uncle," actually *lowering* tobacco taxes, when – if the health of the nation's young people were any concern – they should be raised. Something must be done.

So you ring for your deputy A-G, who comes in, along with a gaggle of legal advisors. "I have some good news," says your deputy, trying to calm you. "Two of our patrol officers just pulled over a minivan for following the car ahead too closely. Lo and behold, the van was stuffed with unstamped cigarettes, which they confiscated. The driver's been charged with 'possession.'"

"Will that search stand up in court?" you ask. "Stopped for tailgating – arrested for contrabanding?" The legal beagles all shake their heads, acknowledging that the defence are sure to make a holiday of that.

"Anyway," you go on, "it doesn't help much to catch some small fry when the big fish keep getting away. Especially when the small fry clam up, too worried about their health to say who gave them the work."

Suddenly, the lightbulb goes on. "We need a public inquiry!" you whoop. "Find me a judge with a good heavy gavel, who's not long on patience, and let's serve subpoenas on the ring leaders and some of the carriers and small shop-owners. Let's hear what they have to say for themselves."

The beagles glance at one another. "No, minister," they mutter. "You can't hold an inquiry into a criminal conspiracy. The Charter…"

"What?" you shout. "The Charter says nothing about inquiries. It's all about prosecutions and trials. For heaven's sake, we've got something going on here that's a danger to society. Let's bring it into the open."

"But minister, sir." The minions remain unconvinced. But to your mind, the solution is obvious. After all, if the sword that Lady Justice wields gets too rusty, she might as well look for other work.

Alas, the old girl might be well advised to update her resumé. Not so long ago, parliaments and legislatures, by the law of the land, had plenary powers to investigate any scams, mistakes or misdeeds whatsoever. They sometimes exercised that power through their own committees, and often by public inquiries. Inquiries are designed to listen and probe, thoroughly and informally. They can also expose, report and recommend.

(Of course, there are also purely research and policy inquiries. But we are not concerned with them here – only with those that may shed light on misconduct or neglect on the part of individuals or corporations.)

Unfortunately, however, within the past 20 years, court decisions have been trimming the sails of inquiries, turning them into expensive futilities. Their usefulness is slowly sinking in a Sargasso Sea of legal entanglements.

The situation has changed dramatically since the sapient words of earlier judges, judges who showed respect for the eyes and ears of elected assemblies. In 1962, for instance, an Ontario Royal Commission had been charged with looking into imputations of criminal activity against certain individuals. In the Court of Appeal, Mr. Justice Laidlaw had these commonsensical words to say about that commission:

> "This inquiry does not in any way resemble a trial in a court of law...No one is charged. It is investigative in character – it can obtain information and draw conclusions in any way and by any means it deems appropriate – it is an effective, efficient, expeditious and practical means of bringing the truth to light."[2]

Laidlaw also quoted the scholarly Justice Middleton who wrote in 1934: "No one should be allowed to burke the fullest investigation." Well, "burked" inquiries are precisely what we have today – not to mention bloated ones. The two seem to travel hand in hand.

The Somalia Farrago

Who can forget the Somalia inquiry, which ran from 1995 to 1997? Sparked by allegations of disciplinary problems in Canada's blue beret United Nations peacekeeping troops, the inquiry's mandate was to investigate the shooting of a Somali civilian who allegedly attempted theft at the troops' base. The story was that some sadistic Canadian soldiers had played a part in the torture-murder of this young man. One soldier was courtmartialled and convicted of manslaughter, but the general response of the military command to these tragic events was thought not to have been rigorous enough.

Lawyers, however, were allowed to swarm all over the hearings, as if they were at a criminal trial (*pace* Justice Laidlaw), threatening to take the Commission to court and arguing that it might – gasp! – find their clients had misconducted themselves and that they thereby could – *sacré Dieu!* – be exposed to social censure, or even end up being sued or charged.

Every witness was accompanied by his or her own personal lawyer, and every general by three. The only people involved who didn't retain lawyers were the lawyers themselves. The Commission spent weeks delving into trivia, such as had a certain press release been altered (as if one had ever been issued unaltered)? Grinding on for two years, spinning its wheels, piling up millions of dollars in costs, the Somalia inquiry began to look more and more like a boondoggle. Finally, the government cut it short, with very little public protest. Its final act was to issue a Report of sweeping condemnations so generalized that afterwards Federal Justice Barbara Reed rejected the whole thing as unsupported.[3]

Who was in control of this out-of-control commission? Not the commissioners. One of them, Peter Desbarais, a well-known and respected journalist, let the cat out of the bag when he wrote of one month of the hearing that:

> "We were required by law to devote the entire month of March to listening to submissions from those who were defending themselves in front of the Inquiry, and hearing their witnesses. We didn't have any choice; lawyers would claim the whole process was unfair, and take us to court immediately."

Oh my! Lawyers holding Royal Commissioners in their gunsights, with lots of ammunition supplied to them by the Courts. Parliament's old right to inquire was well and truly waylaid.

A Refrigerator Puts the Freeze on Inquiries

Ironically, the biggest crimp in crime inquiries' power resulted from some rather commonplace political hanky-panky. In 1988, one Patricia Starr of Toronto was said to have engaged in influence peddling. Starr's women's group had apparently given a refrigerator to one of then-Ontario Premier Bill Peterson's assistants and also painted his house. What's more, some of the group's political contributions came perilously close to bribery. (It must be asked about the refrigerator: Was it big enough to be a bribe? Or small enough to be a gift?)

In the subsequent political furor, the beset premier opted for a public inquiry. Mindful of court precedents, however, he made sure its terms of reference forbade any "expression of opinion" about anyone's likely criminal responsibility. Still, even this hobbled inquiry failed to pass muster in the Supreme Court.[4] It would, said the judges, come too close to unearthing criminal acts. It might, God forbid, even identify criminals.

Let us suppose, in passing, that Premier Peterson had referred the Starr imbroglio to the Legislative Committee on Privileges. That committee, by ancient prerogative, has an unfettered authority to protect the democratic process by compelling witnesses, digging up facts and imposing jail or other penalties. Had the committee been allowed to sift through the evidence, the right of Canada's provincial legislatures to expose and punish lawbreakers might have survived court scrutiny. Alas, we can only speculate.[5]

The *Starr* decision tore a hole in the long-established authority of the provinces granted by Section 92/14 of the 1867 Constitution. And it shredded the power of both federal and provincial commissions of inquiry by enunciating the following specious propositions:

- First, it picked fault with the Terms of Reference in *Starr,* which had named the individuals and the Society to be looked into. There seemed to be some concern that actually naming names could result in bruised feelings! Never mind that the press had been full of the names for weeks.

- Next, the Court found that the inquiry's terms of reference outlined the activities to be investigated in language too close to words describing some Criminal Code offences. Could the Government of Ontario not afford a thesaurus?

- Finally, the Court halted the inquiry on the ground that a police investigation was going on at the same time. These servants of the Legislature were indeed carrying on with work they were paid to do. Apparently, their masters, the legislators, must therefore quit the field. Could the Court have felt too much might come to light? As if Truth were ever in oversupply.

Seeing the trouble to come, Madam Justice L'Heureux-Dubé dissented, to her great credit. The *Starr* inquiry, she wrote, supported the public right to expect integrity in government. As for the "names named," it gave them a chance to clear their blemishes, if they could. And, she added, "the mere fact that charges might be laid is far too fragile a hook on which to hang a Charter violation."

Gone Are the Days

Let us journey back through time to the early 1950s, when black thunderclouds hung over the city of Vancouver. The city's Chief Constable, one Walter Mulligan, stood accused of evil doings – splitting bribes with his gambling squad and taking a monthly retainer from a vice lord. Stormy weather indeed – but a made-to-order public inquiry protected the populace from any stray bolts of lightning.

Mulligan had stood straight and tall as a telephone pole when he'd addressed admiring service-club members, and had ridden high in the saddle at civic parades. He was known as a stickler for law and order, not to mention spit and polish. Until a young lawyer (your author), acting for the police union, had the ruling overturned, Mulligan's officers were under instructions never to doff their tunics during hot weather.

Mulligan's good-guy facade began to crumble, however. Despite the day's Draconian liquor laws, everyone brown-bagged their booze to stow under the table at clubs and restaurants with impunity. Brothels operated openly on the waterfront, and detectives expected their usual Christmas bottle, not only from criminal lawyers but also from the lawyers' clients too. Officers moonlighted as doormen at bookie joints; some blind pigs were raided regularly, while other were not, based upon their relative generosity to the Policeman's Benevolent Fund; and the occasional mysterious body would be deposited in a golf-course bunker.

Then came the newspaper's screaming headlines: "Policemen on the take," "Vancouver becoming hop-head heaven" "Bribes paid for Chief's country love-nest" and so on.

Thanks to this sort of publicity, a new attorney-general replaced the look-the-other-way fellow, and a public inquiry was ordered. Reginald Tupper, a law professor, was named sole commissioner. The hearings, however, soon turned into a parody of *Dragnet*. The bad cops suddenly came down with amnesia, while the remorseful good ones shot themselves. The Chief skipped to Los Angeles before testifying, to become an impressive limo dispatcher at the airport there, returning only after the time limits on the charges against him had run out.

Tupper (although widely derided as "not knowing where the Court House is") ran a tight ship. He compelled testimony, sparing no one, and reported the Chief was "capable but corrupt," that he "took bribes" and that the "degeneration of his character arose from a liaison," presumably with some scarlet woman.

The inquiry had been a felicitous exercise. Within two months, the air had been cleansed and the hookworm of corruption cauterized. Citizens had been both enlightened and titillated, and feelings of great civic solidarity blossomed. Who would want to fit inquiries of such social utility with cement overshoes? Alas, that's what the courts have done.

Putting a Gangland Lord on the Spot

It was 1977, and Nicolo di Orio had no wish to be where he was, in front of a commissioner appointed to look into organized crime in Montreal. The commission's report and transcripts of evidence would go to the prosecutor's office. Like it or not, Nicolo had to be there. Subpoenaed to testify about his gang associations, he took the stand, swore the oath and gave his name. But he refused to answer any questions. His stubborn silence won him a year in jail for contempt.

A whole year! And not even handed down by a judge. Not even by a coroner holding an inquest into some unnatural death. Just some so-called commissioner. Nicolo's lawyers advised a constitutional challenge and enthusiastically obeyed his instructions to take it all the way. The Supreme Court was not so enthusiastic, holding that the inquiry was a legitimate exercise of the authority of a government concerned about public safety. Nicolo's sentence stuck.[6]

In the judgement, Chief Justice Bora Laskin described the commission as "a State-sponsored inquiry by a public tribunal with compulsory and punitive power against those refusing to cooperate in its proceedings." The court majority added that the commission "was a function of a provincial government (under the Constitution's administration of justice section) to investigate crime and identify criminals." If that meant some charges would be laid in the criminal courts, so be it. Of course, any accused going to court would have all the procedural safeguards.

The court left the advisability of holding the inquiry up to the provincial government. In the early 1970s, Montreal's organized criminals had driven their unorganized counterparts off the front pages. Tabloid headlines screamed of gangs running dope, prostitution, gambling, loan-sharking and shake-downs and bribing officials, while the Law looked helplessly on. Justice couldn't touch the well-insulated mob bosses, who left the dirty work to lowly henchmen. Witnesses were stricken with fits of amnesia in the box. Squealers disappeared.

The provincial inquiry had certainly put Nicolo on the spot. Of course, under the Canada Evidence Act, what he said couldn't be used directly against him in court. But what he said would give the police clues to follow, putting Nicolo and his buddies in jeopardy. If he lied on the stand, chances were he'd go down for perjury. Even silence would convey something, not to mention taking him out of circulation for a term.

Such inquiries are clearly a useful supplement to ordinary law enforcement procedures. But, alas, they're now a thing of the past. Since Nicolo paid for his silence with a year in the hoosegow, court precedents have drawn the teeth of crime inquiries. No longer can they "identify criminals" or turn up evidence that might incriminate some individual or organization. The courts have posted a no-trespassing sign – "stay off our turf."

To my mind, this is an inauspicious omen. While gangs wax in power and viciousness, the law's ability to check them wanes. The tentacles of organized crime and its international affiliates now reach across Canada, involved in everything from smuggling illegal aliens to counterfeiting credit cards to trafficking in the gall bladders of slaughtered bears. Murderous gang wars erupt over territory; in 1993 and 1994 in Montreal, 25 people were killed in an 18-month period, including an 11-year-old boy playing too close to a gangland bombing.

A Barn Burner

Another decision pre-dating *Starr* involved a crime that seems to have been rather more disorganized than organized. After the 1970 "October Crisis" in Québec, the air crackled with tension. The RCMP Security Service persevered in trying to track down their men, a small clutch of violent separatists. "You are harassing our citizens," complained the Québec government. Implying that the Mounties' actions were like those of SS officers run amok, it established a commission to investigate them. The commission's terms of reference alleged, *inter alia,* that rogue undercover cops had set fire to a barn and had broken into the home of one Louise Vaudrel and stolen her handbag.

The question of this commission's legality went to the Supreme Court,[7] which found that it was a probe into "specific criminal activities allegedly committed by members of the RCMP." But the commission's authority was upheld, with the Court ruling that its mandate was a valid exercise of provincial powers. Nothing could be clearer. But nothing would have been more thoroughly upset by the later *Starr* decision. Faced with that precedent, the Court would have been forced to arrive at the opposite opinion – if they arrived at an opinion at all. Thus, one possible form of constraint upon excessive or unreasonable measures that may or may not have been adopted by agents of the State would have been denied.

Nothing but the *Starr* decision could do more to disarm democratic government, confronted as it is (and will be even more), not only with criminal conspiracies but with terrorist plots stemming from racial, religious or political hatreds.

The Air India Catastrophe

No matter how horrendous the criminal conspiracy, the courts now stand in the way of a public inquiry. On June 23, 1985, a man with an orange turban paid $3,005 in cash at Vancouver International Airport for tickets on Air India flight 182, bound for India via Toronto. He did not board the plane, but checked luggage onto it. A time-bomb exploded over the Irish Sea, killing all of the 329 passengers and crew. The same day, another man checked luggage onto a flight to India via Japan. He, too, did not board. An explosion killed the baggage handlers at Tokyo's Narita Airport.

By now, more than a decade later, the RCMP's Disaster Force has spent more than $20 million investigating the bombings. Despite their offer of a $1 million reward, and their determination of six suspects (one of them dead), murder charges are still pending. Worse, anguish and anxiety still affect the bereaved families and the Indo-Canadian community. But, thanks to the *Starr* decision, which ruled out a public inquiry into any specific crime, calls for a full inquiry into this crime have been in vain. Such an inquiry would name names, compel testimony, perhaps even finger culprits – all no-nos. What a change in the law since poor Nicolo di Orio faced the music.

Further, Canada's Solicitor-General has raised a related objection to an Air India inquiry. If it were allowed to proceed, he has maintained, any information it produced would likely be inadmissible in court.

But why shouldn't the inquiry testimony be available in an ensuing trial? Would it not assist the trial in helping refine and focus the points in contention? Would it not further the search for truth? How could its use be unfairly oppressive to the accused and their lawyers at trial? They would have the opportunity, once more, to confront and cross-examine adverse witnesses, to contradict or explain as best they could any damaging evidence or admissions.

Such a public inquiry would serve several objectives. It would let the public know who or what may have put human life in jeopardy, much as a coroner's inquest does. It would check unfounded rumours and suspicions and reassure the public that all reasonable precautions will be taken against a reoccurrence. And it would save time and money in the courts.

Sir Charles Gordon, the distinguished former Clerk of the British Parliament, told me that English courts defer to Parliament the right to institute inquiries of all sorts. However, by tradition, Parliament respects the courts' final right to convict or acquit any accused person. Why cannot such common sense and civility reign in our country?

Death of a Princess

When Diana, Princess of Wales, died in that famous crash in the streets of Paris in August 1997, criminal acts may have been to blame. Ten paparazzi armed with cameras had been speeding after the couple's car. Had they displayed a depraved indifference to human life? Had they, or others, failed to stop and render Good Samaritan assistance, as French law obliges them to do? The Paris magistrates at once launched a criminal inquiry – their usual practice in such a case, although no doubt this particular fatality received special time and attention from the authorities. Diana's death had touched millions, and the world was watching. The French know, as well as any people, that courts of justice, along with elected assemblies, are the great theatres of democracy.

Everyone remotely connected to the Princess' accident was summoned peremptorily to the *Palais de Justice.* Had any pleaded other plans, he or she would have found a *gendarmerie* escort, kindly provided by a judge. Under French law, reluctant witnesses can be held incommunicado for up to 48 hours. But all those involved knew that and came forward voluntarily. In front of a judge and under oath, they were closely questioned. Some brought along a lawyer – quite permissible – but none dared to advise their clients, "Don't answer that question," for fear of being bastilled. The same fate would await any advocate found to have planted words in a client's mouth.

As for the notion of someone refusing to answer on the grounds one might be incriminated – *Incroyable! Bizarre!* Can any reasonable person maintain that French citizens' rights are thus severely compromised or curtailed? Or that Canadians' rights to justice are amplified by being under no such compulsion to participate in an orderly search for truth and justice? Unlike we Canadians, who are well and truly Chartered, the French do, it seems, fondly believe that, as the Gilbert and Sullivan ditty goes, their laws are indeed the "true embodiment of everything that's excellent."

A Salutary Inquiry

Let us now turn to a recent quest for truth, where Justice Sam Hughes, in the public interest, managed to sail past the Charter rocks. I refer to the grievous instances of sexual abuse at the Mt. Cashel orphanage in Newfoundland. Between 1971 and 1976, members of a teaching order, the Christian Brothers, committed gross sexual assaults upon young boys in their charge. Wisely, though tardily, the provincial government instituted an inquiry under Hughes, a sage owl and a retired Ontario justice. Wide publicity attended his inquiry, and subsequent criminal trials resulted in convictions on 11 counts of assault.

Miraculously, the Hughes hearings proceeded without constitutional challenge. Only later, during the trials, was its right to delve into criminality questioned – unsuccessfully. The Newfoundland Court of Appeal "distinguished" the *Starr* case, holding that the Mt. Cashel inquiry had been essential to determine how the justice system had responded to the boys' complaints.

You have to wonder how this could have been done without assessing the validity of the complaints.[8] Of course, courts are unduly skittish about using evidence not established within their own processes. Government, too, until recently, did not share information amongst departments. Now, however, facts about a disturbed youngster, say, are shared amongst health, social services, labour, education and attorney-general departments. In the end, the courts concluded that the natural desire of Newfoundlanders to learn the facts of the case, and their expectation of appropriate retribution, had been satisfied.

One objection to the Hughes inquiry was that the pre-trial publicity it generated negated the right of the accused to fair trials. However, the Court of Appeal rejected this objection, saying care had been taken in jury selection to eliminate prejudiced jurors. In addition, the trial judge had clearly admonished the jurors to render their verdicts only upon testimony heard in court.

Surely an informed juror, one who may have followed news reports about an inquiry, can decide impartially on the evidence. If he or she is aware of evidence later found inadmissible in court, then the judge should be able to explain why that evidence cannot be considered – if there are, as there should be, good reasons for its exclusion. The uninformed, uninterested juror is far worse, bringing to court ill-founded biases and gossip.

Moreover, court publication bans are seldom in the interests of justice. If reporting is biased or distorted, it can be countered with the summary penalties of contempt of court. It was a mistake, in the Bernardo case, to bar reporting of Karla Homolka's plea-bargained sentencing hearing. Secrecy only breeds suspicions and infringes the public's right to know under the Charter – not to mention providing grist for the Internet's mills.

Martensville: Adversarial Shortcomings

Allegations of sexual abuse in a day-care home in Martensville, Saskatchewan, represent another instance where an inquiry would have benefitted the criminal proceedings. Without one, more than 100 charges of child abuse were laid against nine accused, including five police officers. The abuse was said to have occurred between 1988 and 1991, when all the children were under the age of 10. The children testified in criminal court with stories sometimes plausible and sometimes fantastic.

The Martensville matter raised questions of the adversarial court system's fitness to probe the truth of such a perplexing web of allegations. How prone are children to either forgetting or imagining sexual details, especially in a court setting? Were the children susceptible to adult influence? Were suggestions planted by the police, prosecutors or others? A sagacious inquiry commissioner could have better determined the facts. He or she could, say, engage a child alone in friendly questions, away from the stage-like formalities of the hearing room, soliciting (although hearsay) the opinions of conscientious neighbours, teachers and social workers.

After all was said and done, of all those charged, the court convicted only one young woman and her brother. On appeal, the woman's conviction was set aside as too doubtful to stand.[9] Her brother later had four convictions dismissed and only two affirmed.

The proceedings throw into doubt the justice system's ability to handle cases where children are victims or witnesses. Without two sides, Crown and defence, each striving for a win, an informal inquiry – by leaving any binding decision of guilt to later court processes – would make certain truth is the quarry.

Sidelining the Community's Right to Know

Another case in point is the 1982 bombing that killed nine miners at the Giant Mine in Yellowknife, Northwest Territories. The murdered miners were "replacing" union workers during a bitter legal strike. No inquiry was held, but a protracted trial eventually found Roger Warren, a union striker, guilty of detonating the explosion.

The decision, however, only partially allayed lingering doubts as to whether others were involved. Uncertainties still plague Yellowknife's residents – uncertainties that might have been laid to rest had an inquiry preceded the trial.

Of course, these days there is no guarantee that an inquiry will be allowed to conduct its business unfettered. Consider the bedevilled fate of the inquiry into the Westray mine disaster.

Deep in the mine shafts in Pictou County, Nova Scotia, pockets of methane gas lay over carpets of coal dust. On May 19, 1992, the gas and dust exploded, killing 26 miners. The catastrophe sent waves of shock and horror through the mining community, the province and the entire country.

Understandably, Nova Scotians wanted to know how this could have happened, and upon whom responsibility rested. Within a week, Justice Peter Richard was appointed as sole Inquiry Commissioner. However, through no fault of his, the public was never to get a full and speedy judicial inquiry. Instead, the inquiry was confined, because of court decisions, to an explanation of the cause of the disaster and the efficacy of the safety regulations. And then, to make matters worse, this limited inquiry was put on hold while charges of criminal negligence slowly wound their way through the courts.

Three years later, by a lucky chance, the Supreme Court allowed the inquiry to proceed.[10] The mine managers on trial had elected to be tried by a judge sitting without a jury. Such a judge, in the High Court's opinion, would have the pluck to pay no attention to what the newspapers say came out at the inquiry. Were a jury to sit, this statement implied, its members could not be counted upon to exhibit such fortitude.

Thus the Westray Inquiry, limited as it was, minding its Ps and Qs as it had, carried on and reported – before hearing any evidence from the company's chief executive officer, Clifford Frame. That worthy fellow was still in the courts, fighting for his "right" not to testify. Now, no one will ever know what was done, or not done, about safety in the company's Toronto board rooms.

Justice Richard did manage to bring down as strong a report as he could, in the circumstances, showing the minimum respect necessary for the nonsensical ruling that he could say what caused the accident but not who was to blame for it.

But then, a bolt from the blue! The court charges that had run interference with the Inquiry for six long years were dropped by the Crown for lack of evidence. What message did that send to the grieving families about the pursuit of truth and justice? As one mother said, "My son was buried in that mine…It's been six years." And as a sister noted, "The justice system is the pits."

The Tainted-Blood Inquiry

Since the early 1980s, thousands of Canadians have become ill or died from the viruses that cause AIDS and hepatitis C because of blood transfusions. A redoubtable commissioner, Justice Horace Krever, was named to explore the calamity. But for 18 months, his hearings were held up while the courts fretted that he might lay too much blame. During that delay, some 200 to 300 victims died. The Supreme Court, in allowing these hearings to go on,[11] spoke through a single designated hitter, Justice Peter Cory. His judgement displayed more tolerance for people's desires to expose and check misconduct. Had some of the heat of public opinion infiltrated the precincts of the courts? At any rate, in 1997, Justice Krever was permitted to name some names, as long as he toned down his language.

Where Are We Now?

If only the courts were to simply overlook the *Starr* decision as an obvious aberration! Instead, they pick paths through and around it. This has left the law concerning inquiries littered with confusions and uncertainties, each one an engraved invitation to lawyers to take some inquiry to court.

Consider these questions:

- Can an inquiry be stopped because the publicity it generates may deprive someone of a "fair" trial? The Court's answer – a firm "perhaps."

- Can an inquiry and court charges go on at the same time? The Court replies with a hesitant "possibly."

- Can a witness who might face charges be compelled to speak at an inquiry? A definite "maybe" is the Court's verdict.

- Can an inquiry work together with police investigations? Can commission counsel assist in drafting the inquiry's report? The Court intones, "Stay tuned."

- When does an inquiry cross a blurred line and become a substitute for a "proper" criminal investigation? "That's hard to say," the Court responds, "but we know this for sure, we don't want another Di Orio-style probe of organized crime, nor any probe of the Air India tragedy."

When is an inquiry in trouble for letting the chips fall where they may? "Never," should be the answer. If a Commissioner thinks someone has broken or bent the law, he or she should be able to say so and refer the matter to prosecutors, who can decide to charge or not to charge. If the Commissioner finds that someone slipped up, he or she should be able to pin the blame. Taking one's lumps is part of life. A cabinet minister dumped loses both altitude and reputation. Someone fired, rightly or wrongly, for mismanagement of company funds, loses social standing. An innocent man finally acquitted in the courts has a reputation to repair as best he can. Taking blame is implicit in freedom of speech, together with a right to talk back.

Underlying these and other uncertainties are the basic judge-made errors. First, it is simply wrong, in law and in common sense, to apply the Charter's "legal rights" section to the conduct of inquiries. Inquiries put no one on trial. They dig, inform, advise; they certainly do not deprive anyone of "life, liberty or security of the person," as Section 7 has it. They can't levy fines, much less imprison.

To appreciate the second error's magnitude, a short civics lesson is in order. Our democracy, as I am sure you know, has two important branches: Her Majesty's judicial branch – our judges, high and low – and Her Majesty's parliamentary branch – our esteemed political hacks. Neither should jump the fence into the other's territory. Getting close to the truth is part of Parliament's job. How else can its members pass good laws, criminal or civil? The courts have no business blinkering the eyes of an elected body, or stuffing its ears. Parliament, and its provincial counterparts, should be free to pursue knowledge in its own way.

If a provincial coroner's court can investigate culpable homicides and turn the transcripts over to a prosecutor – as it can – how come public inquiries get jumped on for, on occasion, ferreting out law-breaking and passing that on? Constitutionally, coroners' inquests and public inquiries are on the same footing. Only one gets hobbled, while the other goes free.

When a government makes a hash of the inquiry process – by appointing biased or weak-kneed commissioners, for instance – press and public let the government know it in short order. The best check, to make inquiries work well, is voter vigilance. The worst is for the courts to make Royal Commissioners feel like Macbeth, that they have been "cabined, cribbed, confined, bound in, to saucy doubts and fears."

Epilogue

S o, Patient Reader, having come this far, you may well be thinking, "Hold! Enough, already!" But sadly, willing away the chronic departure from common sense and natural justice besetting our courts is not enough. With every day that passes, more bitter fruit of the Supreme Court's errant judgements comes to light.

As I write this piece, the day's newspaper carries a front page story of a suspect in double murder on the first weekend of 1999. The suspect had been on the nation's front pages once before, in 1992, when the Supreme Court of Canada overturned a 1985 judgement that had found him and another teenager guilty of the brutal murder of an 83-year-old man. The pair, who at trial claimed they had killed their victim because they believed that doing so would give them "superhuman" mental abilities, were held by the Higher Court to be not guilty by reason of insanity, not because they did not think their murder was illegal, but because they did not think at the time it was *morally* wrong. Four months after the Court rendered its judgement, the young man now implicated in the present-day murder was also released from psychiatric care.

Manitoba's justice minister at the time, Jim McRae, asked, when he heard the judgement: "How is the public assured that the public safety is being looked after?" Nearly a decade later, that poignant question still echoes, unanswered, through Canada's courtrooms.

I wish not to be simply a Cassandra, spouting doom and gloom to no effect. I have exposed faults in our criminal justice system, and I have proffered some suggestions as to correcting them.

166

On October 19, 1997, the Chief Justice of Canada spoke to a conference of criminal lawyers in Ottawa and denounced public criticism of some of his Court's decisions as "uninformed and outrageous."[1] His words met a warm reception from the lawyers present. Could they possibly have a vested interest in laws complex enough to obscure truth?

With respect, to call the questions of interested citizens "uninformed" is somewhat high-handed − as if we couldn't tell bad sense from good. Public debate is a democratic right, the essential ingredient in any recipe for a healthier society. In any event, public scrutiny of criminal justice is needed now as never before.

To my mind − and I hope you agree − reform of Canada's criminal justice system can't come too quickly. There's no need to jettison the Charter's Legal Rights − just a need to interpret these words wisely. Some constitutional amendments may also be necessary, along with more liberal and careful use of the "notwithstanding" clause.

Reserving two or three places on the Supreme Court for (dare I say it?) non-lawyers would be a smart move. A few eminent Canadians from the fields of history, economics, sociology, psychology, would doubtless improve the quality − the *humanity* − of judgements. They could be selected after hearings by the Commons' Justice Committee to serve limited terms, their purpose to ascertain the good sense and social consequence of Court rulings.

And what about jurors? According to one vulnerable court watcher (who shall remain nameless), they understandably rebel at their exclusion from court while points of law are debated and resent being treated as "necessary idiots who could not be trusted with an explanation." They also complain that being denied access to information about previous convictions reduces their ability to decide honestly on guilt or innocence.

Juries need to be informed of the defence case at the outset, so they know the relevance (if any) of the questions asked and the evidence called. They are distrustful of pompous barristers, suspicious of police evidence in the light of miscarriage of justice and angry at the inefficiency of criminal trials with so much time wasted while documents and witnesses are found.

It must be obvious by now that, despite my life in the law, I lean in the direction of the average citizen's right − and duty − to adopt a more direct role in ensuring that justice is done. Some would argue that the most effective means to this end is vigilantism − an opinion which I reject outright.

Instead I believe the answer lies in thoughtful reconsideration by our elected representatives (maybe even by the courts – who knows?) of redressing the current imbalance between rights of the accused and rights of all the rest of us – an imbalance so badly skewed by the courts' interpretation of our Charter of Rights and Freedoms.

Let me close with words from a speech given by the no-nonsense Madam Justice L'Heureux-Dubé (by no means the only sensible person in legal ranks), on September 23, 1997, in Ottawa:[2]

> "When an attacker or murderer is acquitted in the name of the regularity of criminal process, it is not only past victims who are ignored, but also future victims who are sacrificed. Rights of the accused can go along with preserving society's capacity to protect its most vulnerable members and exposure of the truth."

Notes

Preface

1 *The Costs of Crime,* study by Profs. Brantingham and Easton, Simon Fraser University, 1998.
2 *The Vancouver Sun,* Oct. 29, 1997.
3 *The Globe and Mail,* April 18, 1998.

Chapter 1

1 Justice Hugo Black, *The Vision* (Boston: Little, Brown, 1966).
2 In a pre-Charter case (*R v Wray*, SCC 1971, SCR 272), the Court upheld the rule that judges could not exclude evidence, even if it brought justice into disrepute.
3 *Miranda v Arizona*, USSC [United States Supreme Court]1966, 384, US 436.
4 *Wigmore on Evidence*, 1961 edition, Vol. 8, p. 31.
5 *R v Seo*, 1988, Ont. C.A., 54 OR (2nd), 593.
6 A reference by Justice Cory in *R v Bernshaw*, 1995, SCC [Supreme Court Cases] (3rd).
7 *R v Mohl*, 1987, Sask. C.A., 34 CCC [Canadian Criminal Cases] (3rd), 435.
8 *R v Prosper*, 1995, SCC 92 CCC (3rd), 353.
9 *R v Bartle*, 1995, SCC 92, CCC (3rd), 289.
10 Reported in *The Globe and Mail,* July 26, 1991.
11 *R v St. Pierre*, 1995, SCC 96 CCC (3rd), 385.
12 See *The Vancouver Sun*, Nov. 15, 1996. Parliament should have the constitutional courage to amend Section 254.3 of the Criminal Code to make it clear that an officer's "reasonable belief" justifies demanding a breath test.
13 Ontario Highway Traffic Act, Section 48.3 (1996); B.C. Motor Vehicle Act, amended 1995.
14 *R v Duguay et al.*, 1985 Ont. C.A., 8 CCC (3rd), 289.
15 *The Law of Evidence in Canada* (Toronto: Butterworths, 1992).
16 *R v Manninen*, 1987, SCC 34 CCC (3rd), 385.
17 *R v Carston*, 1990, NBCA 51 CCC (3rd), 237.
18 *R v Barnes*, 1991, SCC 63, CCC (3rd), 1.
19 *Clarkson v The Queen*, 1986, SCC 25 CCC (3rd), 207.
20 Quoted in *B.C. Report*, Oct. 17, 1994.
21 *R v Tzimos*, 1993, Ont. Crim. Conv. 5210-05.
22 *R v Corbett*, 1993, Ont. Crim. Conv., 5210-09.
23 *R v Robert*, 1998, BCCA 132, DLR (4th), 422.

Chapter 2

1 *R v Durette et al.,* 1992, Ont. CA, 72 CCC (3rd) 421.
2 *The Vancouver Sun,* January 15, 1995.

3   *R v Rodenbush,* 1985, BCCA, 21 CCC (3rd), 423.
4   *R v Monney,* 1997, Ont. CA, 120 CCC (3rd) 99.
5   *The Globe and Mail,* November 21, 1997.
6   *R v Pizzardi,* 1994. Ont. CA 17 OR (3rd), 623.
7   Quoted by Joey Thompson, *The Province* (Vancouver), April 24, 1996.
8   *R v Pohoretsky,* 1987, 1 SCR 945.
9   *R v Hieronymi,* 1995, Ontario C.A., Ont. D. Crim., 5210-13.
10 *R v Roy,* 1997, Quebec CA 117, CCC (3rd), 245.
11 *R v Shallow,* 1997 Ont. Prov. Court, Ont D. Crim, 260.

Chapter 3

1   *Hamlet,* Act III, Scene 1.
2   Speech to the Laval Chamber of Commerce, reported in *The Globe and Mail,* April 19, 1995.
3   *"Trends in Justice Spending,"* Canadian Centre for Justice Statistics.
4   *The Globe and Mail,* November 23, 1994. The Court said these delays were "institutional," suggesting the solution was to throw more money at the problem.
5   *R v Alekseev,* Shephard, J., 1992, BC ULD, 86.
6   *R v Gray et al.,* 1993, BCCA, 79 CCC (3rd), 332.
7   *R v Gray et al.,* 1995, 43 CR (4th) 52, BCSC.
8   *R. v Stinchcome,* 1992, SCC 68 CCC (3rd).
9   *R v Carosella,* 1997, SCC 112 CCC (3rd) 289.
10 See *R v O'Connor,* 1995, SCC 103, CCC (3rd) 1, page 79.
11 *R v Zito,* 1995, 94 CCC (3rd) 477 (Ont CA).
12 *R v Gray,* 1997, Ont. Gen. Div., Ont. Crimn. Cases, 260.
13 *R v Alain,* 1992, BCCA, 18 Weekly Criminal Bulletin, 198.

Chapter 4

1   *R v Vaillancourt,* 1988, SCC 39, CCC (3rd), 118.
2   *The Vision,* H. Black, Little Brown, Boston, 1966.
3   See *Report of the US Senate Judicial Committee,* May 25, 1995.
4   *Blackborn v A-G,* 1983, Chancery 77 at page 89.
5   Re Public Sector Pay Reduction, 1997, SCC 118, CCC (3rd), 193.
6   *The Vancouver Sun,* July 18, 1998.
7   *R v Bernard,* 1989, SCC 45, CCC (3rd) 1.
8   See Dickson, CJC and Lamer J, in the *Bernard* case.
9   *R v Penno,* 1991, SCC 59 CCC (3rd), 344.
10 *R v Parks,* 1992, SCC 75 CCC (3rd) 287.
11 *R v Daviault,* 1995, SCC 93 CCC (3rd) 21.
12 Section 33 of the Charter allows Parliament and legislatures to enact laws "notwithstanding" the Charter's Legal Rights provisions, though only for renewable five-year periods.

13 *1995 Statutes of Canada,* Ch. 32. Intoxication remains (under Daviault) a defence to other general-intent offences.

14 *Supreme Court of B.C. newsletter,* April, 1998.

15 Section 16 of the Criminal Code, 1992. A defendant detained under this section is subject to restraint under conditions set by Provincial Review Boards, with an appeal to the courts.

16 See *R vs Sullivan,* 1995, BCCA 96, CCC (3rd), 135. The Appeal Court, on the evidence at hand, upheld the jury's finding of "mental disorder."

Chapter 5

1 *R v I (L.R.),* SCC 1993, 4 SCR, 504.

2 *People v Defore;* Justice Benjamin N. Cardozo, 1926, 242 N.Y. 13 at 21.

3 According to a report by J. Oaks in the *University of Chicago Law Review* (1989, p. 678).

4 Julian W. Mack, *The Juvenile Court,* 1909 23, *Harvard Law Review,* 104.

5 *R v R.A.D.,* Alberta Court of Appeal, 1988, 61 Alta L.R. (2nd) 29.

6 *R v H.,* 1985, Alberta Youth Court, 43 Alta L.R. (2nd) 250.

7 *R v Johnson,* 1997, Peterborough Prov. Div., Ont. D Crim., 12-97.

8 *R v J* (J.T.) 1991, SCC 59, CCC (3rd) 1.

9 Douglas Broome, B.C. Youth Court Adviser, quoted in *The Vancouver Sun,* March 7, 1995. The U.S. and Poland take the gold and silver medals.

10 *R v J.M.A.,* 1987, Man. CA, 46 Man. R (2nd), 309. The lad was acquitted thanks to the Charter – his guardian had not sufficiently impressed upon him that he was not obliged to answer police questions.

11 Quoted in *The Advocate* (Vancouver Bar, Spring, 1996)

12 Quoted in *The Vancouver Sun,* Oct. 21, 1996.

13 *In R v Oakes,* SCC 1986, 50 CR (3rd) 1, Chief Justice C.J.C. Dickson used this phrase when referring to the "presumption of innocence."

14 Hard cases can make bad law. There was a mandatory minimum sentence in the Code that applied to any trafficking, regardless of the person, his record, or the gravity of the offence. Such minimums should be struck down under Charter Sec. 12 as "cruel and unusual punishment."

15 Charter, Section 1.

16 *R v Downey,* SCC 1992, 72 CCC (3rd) 1.

Chapter 6

1 *R v Castellani,* BCCA, 1967, 3 CCC 312; also BCCA, 1969, 1 CCC 327, and 1970, 4 CCC 287.

2 *R v Hebert,* SCC 1990, 57 CCC (3rd), 1.

3 *Rothman v Q,* 1981, 1 SCR 640

4 *R v Brown,* 1992, SCC 83, CCC (314), 129; Madam Heureux-Dubé dissenting.

5 *R v Calder,* 1997, SCC 105, CCC (3rd), 1

6 *R v François,* 1994, SCC 91 CCC (3rd), 289.

7   *R v Genaille,* 1997, Man. C.A., 116 CCC (3rd), 459.
8   Jeremy Bentham, *Rationale of Judicial Evidence,* p. 528.
9   *R v Eden,* 1970, Ont. C.A., 3 CCC 280.
10 *The Province,* May 5, 1994.
11 *R v B (J.N.),* 1989, Man. C.A., 48 CCC (3rd), 71.
12 *R v S (R.T.),* SCC 96, CCC (3rd), 1
13 *R v Crawford,* 1995, SCC 96, CCC (3rd), 481.
14 *R v Noble,* 1997, SCC 114 CCC (3rd), 385.
15 *Russell on Crime,* 5th edition, Vol. 1, p. 292.
16 *The Vancouver Sun,* July 28, 1995, p. A1.
17 In *Palko v Connecticut,* 1937, 302, U.S. 319 at p. 326.
18 Voltaire, *Zadig,* 1747. Chapter 6.
19 Re *Milgaard,* SCC 1992, 72 CCC (3rd) 280.
20 *R v Hebert,* above.
21 "Justice probably swifter in Britain than in Canada," *The Vancouver Sun,* July 7, 1998.
22 *R v Babinski,* 1992, SCC 67 CCC (3rd) 187.
23 *R v Lee,* 1996, Ont. D. Crim., 06-96.
24 *R v Ross,* 1989, SCC 46 CCC (3rd) 129.
25 *R v Michalatos,* 1993, Ont. Crim. Conv. 5210

Chapter 7

1   *R v Collins,* SCC 1987, 33 CCC (3rd), 1.
2   *Justice Statistics,* 85 00L.
3   *Rochin v California,* USSC, 1952, 347 US 128.
4   *R v Wilson,* 1994, BCCA 29 CR (4th), 302.
5   *R v Klimchuk,* 1991, BCCA, 67 CCC (3rd), 385.
6   *R v Belnavis and Lawrence,* 1997, SCC 118, CCC (3rd), 405.
7   *R v Castlake,* 1998, SCC 121, CCC (3rd) 97.
8   *R v Kokesch,* SCC 1990, 61 CCC (3rd), 207.
9   *R v Wong,* 1991 SCC 60 CCC (3rd), 460
10 *R v Borden,* SCC 1995, 92 CCC (3rd) 404.
11 *R v Stillman,* 1997, 113 CCC (3rd) 321.
12 From *Hamlet,* Act I, Scene 3.
13 *R v S (c),* 1997, Toronto, Provincial Court of Ontario, D. Crim. 11-97.
14 *R v Nielson,* 1985, Man. C.A., 16 CCC (3rd) 39.

Chapter 8

1   *R v Wholesale Travel,* 1991, SCC 154.
2   1984, 2 SC 12, 145.
3   *The Vancouver Sun,* February 2, 1995.
4   For reported references to the Bennett case, see 1991 BCSC 82 DLR 129,

and 1992 BCCA 95 DLR 341. Motion for Leave to Appeal to the Supreme Court was refused without reasons.

5 *The Vancouver Sun,* February 2, 1995.

6 *The Globe and Mail,* December 22, 1994.

7 Ibid.

8 *B.C. Securities Commission v Branch,* 1995, SCC 97 CCC (3rd), 505.

9 See B.C. Securities Commission decision, August 28, 1996, COR#96/170, 186 pages. Doman and R.J. have appealed this decision. Bill Bennett did not, saving some fees and allowing him to "coat-tail." They got nothing substantial on this appeal.

10 Cavanagh, J., *Southam Inc. and Thomson Newspapers v Hunter,* 1982, Alta. Q.B. 68 CCC (2nd) 356.

11 *Re: Southam Inc.,* 1985, SCC 14, CCC (3rd), 97.

12 *The New York Times,* November 13, 1996.

13 *See Norwest Holst v Secretary of State of Trade,* 1978, Ch. 201.

14 *R v Print Three,* 1986, 10 OAC 220 Ont. C.A.

15 *R v Miller,* 1986, 3 F.C. (C.A.) 291.

16 *R v Ozubko,* 1986, Man. C.A., 33 DLR (4th), 714.

Chapter 9

1 United States Supreme Court Justice Louis Brandeis, 1932.

2 Re *Ontario Crime Commission,* 1962, Ontario Reports, 872. Laidlaw, J.A., was dissenting. The other two appeal judges upheld the commission, but said an impugned person should be allowed to call evidence and cross-examine.

3 *The Vancouver Sun,* April 29, 1998.

4 *Starr v Holden,* 1990, SCC 55, CCC (3rd), 472.

5 This is an ancient common law parliamentary prerogative.

6 *Di Orio and Fontaine v The Warden of the Common Jail of Montreal,* 1977, SCC 33, CCC (2nd), 289.

7 *A.G. (Canada) and Keable v A.G. (Québec),* 1979, SCC 43 CCC (2nd), 49.

8 *R v English,* 1994, CCC (3 rd), 511.

9 *The Vancouver Sun,* Oct. 17, 1997.

10 *Phillips et al v Nova Scotia,* 1995, SCC 98 CCC (3rd) 20.

11 *Canada (A.G.) v Inquiry on Blood System,* 1997, SCC, 152, DLR (4th), 13.

Epilogue

1 *The Vancouver Sun,* Oct. 20, 1997.

2 *The Vancouver Sun,* Sept. 24, 1998.

Index